PENGUIN
I KEEP VIGIL OF RUDRA

H.S. Shivaprakash is a well-known poet, playwright and translator from Karnataka. His translations and adaptations of Shakespeare are widely staged. He has also translated major European, Latin American and African poets into Kannada and some of the best-known Kannada and Tamil poets into English. He is the winner of the Sangeet Natak Akademi Award for playwriting and four best book prizes of the Karnataka Sahitya Akademi for poetry and translations. A former editor of the translations journal *Indian Literature*, Shivaprakash is an honorary fellow of the School of Letters, University of Iowa, and a specialist in Indian devotional traditions. He is currently professor, Theatre and Performance Studies, Jawaharlal Nehru University, New Delhi.

I KEEP VIGIL OF RUDRA

The Vachanas

Translated with an introduction by
H.S. Shivaprakash

PENGUIN BOOKS

PENGUIN BOOKS
Published by the Penguin Group
Penguin Books India Pvt. Ltd, 11 Community Centre, Panchsheel Park, New Delhi 110 017, India
Penguin Group (USA) Inc., 375 Hudson Street, New York, New York 10014, USA
Penguin Group (Canada), 90 Eglinton Avenue East, Suite 700, Toronto, Ontario, M4P 2Y3, Canada (a division of Pearson Penguin Canada Inc.)
Penguin Books Ltd, 80 Strand, London WC2R 0RL, England
Penguin Ireland, 25 St. Stephen's Green, Dublin 2, Ireland (a division of Penguin Books Ltd)
Penguin Group (Australia), 250 Camberwell Road, Camberwell, Victoria 3124, Australia (a division of Pearson Australia Group Pty Ltd)
Penguin Group (NZ), 67 Apollo Drive, Rosedale, North Shore 0632, New Zealand (a division of Pearson New Zealand Ltd)
Penguin Group (South Africa) (Pty) Ltd, 24 Sturdee Avenue, Rosebank, Johannesburg 2196, South Africa

Penguin Books Ltd, Registered Offices: 80 Strand, London WC2R 0RL, England

First published by Penguin Books India 2010

Copyright © H.S. Shivaprakash 2010
Introduction © H.S. Shivaprakash 2010

All rights reserved

10 9 8 7 6 5 4 3 2 1

ISBN 9780143063575

Typeset in Bembo by Eleven Arts, New Delhi
Printed at Anubha Printers, Noida

This book is sold subject to the condition that it shall not, by way of trade or otherwise, be lent, resold, hired out, or otherwise circulated without the publisher's prior written consent in any form of binding or cover other than that in which it is published and without a similar condition including this condition being imposed on the subsequent purchaser and without limiting the rights under copyright reserved above, no part of this publication may be reproduced, stored in or introduced into a retrieval system, or transmitted in any form or by any means (electronic, mechanical, photocopying, recording or otherwise), without the prior written permission of both the copyright owner and the above-mentioned publisher of this book.

To my guru of gurus
Shree Shivalinga Mahaswamy,
A name without form
Fragrance without colour
And
Light
Everywhere

Contents

Acknowledgements	ix
Introduction	xi
Abbreviations of the Kannada Source Texts	lxxix
The Path: Vachanas	1
The Path: I Saw This Wonder	7
The Path: Ugh! This Empty Show of the World	39
The Path: Labour	85
The Path: Journey	103
The Destination: Union	151
Select Bibliography	171

Acknowledgements

'Without togetherness, no joy of joys'
—Akkamahadevi

Though I have been working on these translations for over twenty-five years, they would not have seen the light of day but for the help and support of many friends and well wishers.

It was the late Professor P. Ramamurthy who suggested I translate vachanas as part of my Ph.D thesis. It was unfortunate that he passed away before seeing it completed. My Ph.D supervisor Professor C.N. Srinath gave me many useful suggestions about translation during my Ph.D years. In those days when the computer was unknown, Sandhya worked very hard to make copies of several drafts of my translations.

My encounter with Professor Daniel Weisbort, former editor of the influential journal, *Poetry in Translation*, at a workshop in Bhopal helped me gain many insights into the art of translation. He also pointed out that after A.K. Ramanujan had introduced vachanas to English readers with his brilliant translations, there was a need for more specialized versions of these texts. He inspired me to rethink my translations.

It was in Iowa city in 2000 that I nearly finalized my translations with the generous help of the young American poet Parker Smothers who was introduced to me by my friend Philip Lutgendorf. This would not be possible had Professor Peter Green not got me invited to the International Writing Workshop that year.

Acknowledgements

My former student, Manu Devadevan, himself a poet and translator of great merit, lent invaluable help in tidying up the translations and the introduction. It was during the course of a discussion with him that it occurred to me that the vachanas should be arranged not author-wise, but in a dialogic fashion.

There is a great tradition of vachana lovers and scholars right from the twelfth century to the present who, by the dint of their hard labour, preserved and prevented the vachana texts from passing into oblivion. After the coming of printing technology, a whole tradition of textual scholars that includes Basavanal, Halakatti, R.C. Hiremath, M.S. Sunkapur, Ja. Cha. Ni., L. Basvaraju, S. Vidyashankar went on trying to improve the existing versions of these texts with their painstaking scholarly labour. Every translator has to acknowledge their enormous labour in making the vachanas available to us in the present form.

When I had almost given up hope of getting my translations published, my friends Mahalakshmi and Rakesh rekindled it, and Ravi Singh offered to publish them. My editors Sivapriya and Anurag have worked on these texts with loving care.

To all the friends I have named above I owe a deep debt of gratitude.

Introduction

> Alas! They make versions of versionless non-version.
> —Allama Prabhu

Historical Context

Medieval Kannada literature spans a period of about seven centuries from the beginning of the twelfth century. However, the borders of this period are sometimes pushed back and forth. For instance, some historians consider Muddanna, the famous poet who saw the birth of the twentieth century, as part of medieval literature whereas the Tatvapadakaras of the eighteenth century are regarded as the precursors of modern Kannada literature. Historically, these centuries saw many dramatic events on the socio-political and cultural frontiers of Karnataka. Among other things, the period saw the fall of the Chalukyas of Kalyana, the meteoric rise and disappearance of the Kalachuryas, and the ups and downs of the Hoysalas of Dorasamudra. These events roughly characterized the political landscape of the first two centuries of the medieval period. The most important event during the later centuries was the setting up and consolidation of the Vijayanagara empire. The rise of the Bahmani sultanate of Bijapur and the emergence of smaller kingdoms and fiefdoms like those of Bidanur, Mysore and of the Keoadi family also took place during this period. Of all these developments, the Kalachurya and Vijayanagara empires made the greatest difference to Kannada language and literature.

Introduction

The Shaiva and Vaishnava bhakti movements that swept across all of Karnataka had a much greater formative influence on the literature of the period than purely political events. Though it would be inaccurate to claim that the period produced only bhakti literature, there is no denying the fact that the bhakti way of seeing pervades the best works of medieval Kannada literature. The positive effects of bhakti were the liberation of language from the artificial conventions of courtly writing that characterized most of the works of the ancient period; the creation of shorter genres of literature like the vachanas and kirtanes, which are more accessible to the common man than long and involved narratives of the previous age. It is no wonder, then, that these changes influenced the content and form of the narrative poetry of the period. The narrative poetry stopped singing praises of kings and emperors by comparing them with mythological figures like Arjuna or Bhima as did the leading poets of the previous age.[1] The heroes of medieval narrative poems were not military heroes any more, but spiritual heroes. The form of narrative poetry also underwent a sea change, thanks to the bhakti movement. The greatest narrative poets of the previous age, with minor exceptions, employed Champu, a genre characterized by Sanskrit metres. The medieval narrative poets resorted to simpler vernacular metres like Shatpadi, Sangatya and Tripadi.

Bhakti movements were not without their negative effects.

---

[1] The celebrated eleventh-century works like Pampa's *Vikramarjunavijayam* and Ranna's *Sahasabhimavijayam* typify this model. These works modelled their patron after mythological characters like Arjuna and Bhima by producing a narrative that was at once a retelling of the Mahabharata and a eulogized account of their patron's glory.

Introduction

Many of the lesser poets took spiteful sectarian propaganda to be the main task of poetry and produced mediocre work. This is a weakness that has at times diluted even the works of otherwise great poets like Basavanna and Harihara. The pervasive influence of the bhakti movements limited the content of literature to the religious. Only the greatest poets of the period like the Vachanakaras and Haridasas at their best, and Kumaravyasa, are free from the stigma of sectarianism.

The overall drama of the medieval Kannada literature was played out against the background of great social and political turbulence. The dynasties that ruled different parts of the land were constantly at war with each other. To make matters worse, there were invasions from the Muslim sultanates of the north. Massacres during war, looting and arson, the weight of heavy taxation—all these added to the burden of the common man. Though bhakti movements attempted to make caste exploitation less severe, they gave rise to bloody conflicts between Shaivas, Vaishnavas, Jainas and Muslims. On the whole, it was a period of endless conflicts, a feature best captured in historical narratives like Nanjundakavi's *Ramanathacharite* produced in the latter half of the medieval period. Given this general background of turbulence, it is small wonder that bhakti exercised irresistible fascination on the minds of common people by offering salvation from the endless suffering of everyday life.

This was also a period during which the bhakti movements, the twelfth-century Sharana movement in particular, challenged caste hierarchy. However, all these developments had no lasting effects on the social structure based, theoretically, on varnashrama dharma. The Vijayanagara emperors, the symbol of the 'pride' of the Kannada people, used such grandiloquent titles as

Gobrahmana Pratipalanacharya (the great protector of cows and Brahmins), Hinduraya Suratrana (the king of Hindus and the life of Brahmins) and Vaidikamarga Samsthapanacharya (the great founder of the Vedic path). On the basis of these titles one may deduce that the duty of the king, theoretically, was to uphold Brahmins, cows and Vedic values. The social structure—consisting of four varnas, eighteen kulas and innumerable castes—was controlled by the Brahmin-Kshatriya-Vaisya combine. Agraharas and Brahmapuris (Brahmin colonies); monasteries and temples; and Banajusanghas (associations of traders and merchants) were the privileged institutions. The rigid caste hierarchy continued to be maintained through various means by the institution of dana or charity,[2] meant only for satpatras (the deserving), which obviously meant Brahmins; by waging barbaric wars against feudatory lords who refused to pay timely tributes; by glorifying the slavish heroism of common people sacrificing their lives for the sake of their lord, and deification of women condemned to perform sati, which are documented in an hyperbolic manner in innumerable monuments like viragallu (hero stones) and mastigallu (chaste-woman stones). The number of castes multiplied throughout the medieval age. In spite of this, the varnashrama order remained theoretically inviolable. The rigidity of varnashrama-based caste rules applied not only to the living, but also to the dying. S. Settar's analysis has persuasively shown that among the people who undertook innumerable voluntary forms of ritual death in conformity to Jaina teachings, all belonged to privileged dwija (twice-born) castes (that is,

---

[2]For a theoretical discussion see Mauss, Marcel, *The Gift: The Form and Reason for Exchange in Archaic Societies,* W.W. Norton, New York/London, 1990.

Brahmin, Kshatriya and Vaisya), except one.[3] Caste privileges affected otherworldly matters too.

The only ways out of such an unassailable fort of dharma were samadhi (absorption in god), moksha (escape from a conditioned existence) and atmarpane (self-immolation of heroes and virtuous women). The literary transformations of the medieval period had to be effected against a backdrop as vicious as this.

The vachana as a form of poetry attained its zenith during the twelfth-century Sharana movement, which ended in political violence and counter-violence. The ruling class had greater material power than Sharana revolutionaries and the scattering of the movement was a setback for the future development of the form.

The efflorescence of the vachanas, however, altered the course of Kannada literature for centuries to come. The revolutionary force of the vachanas was assimilated into the hegemonic values of medieval society. This socio-political process is reflected in the literature of the succeeding centuries by the so-called followers of the Sharana tradition. The successors of the twelfth-century Sharanas gradually rose to a privileged position in the Vijayanagara empire, particularly during the rule of Praudadevaraya.

From the thirteenth to the sixteenth centuries, vachana writing virtually disappeared. However, the Virashaivas, who had inherited the values of the vachana movement, found a rallying point under the patronage of the rulers of Vijayanagara. They had before them the model of attempts at the reintegration of the works and scriptures of classical Hinduism undertaken by

[3]S. Settar, *Pursuing Death: Philosophy and Practice of Voluntary Termination of Life*, 1990, Karnataka University, Dharwar, p. 230.

Introduction

Brahmin sages and pandits from the middle of the fourteenth century onwards, following the threat of Muslim invasion. A similar attempt at the consolidation of Virashaiva lore and vachana canon was undertaken during the fifteenth century by the Virashaiva priestly class. For them, the twelfth-century Sharana movement was no more an immediate reality. It was a glorious memory, a myth. They carried out a reinterpretation of the myth through scholarly endeavours like collections, anthologies and commentaries on vachana texts. Mahalinga (circa 1430 AD), Kalmatada Prabhudevaru (circa 1430 AD), Gubbi Mallannarya (early part of the fifteenth century), Channaviracharya (sixteenth century AD) and Singalada Siddhabasava (circa 1600 AD) expressed their theological erudition in their collections, selections and anthologies of vachana texts purely from the standpoint of bhakti. Singalada Siddhabasava produced sophisticated commentaries on the Bedagina vachanas in the light of the Shakti Vishishtadvaita Vedanta. What is characteristic of all these scholarly endeavours is the over emphasis on the theological and metaphysical aspects of the vachanas and the total exclusion of their socio-political and existentialist implications.

The most impressive achievement in vachana scholarship during the period was the compilation of the versions of *Shoonya Sampadane*. The first version was compiled by Shivaganaprasadi Mahadevaiah (circa 1400 AD). He conceived the overall pattern of *Shoonya Sampadane*, which was adhered to by later compilers with a few inclusions, and omissions of details. Mahadevaiah ordered the sayings of various vachanakaras in the form of philosophical dialogues and linked them through passages of prose narration and description. He must have taken the hint from the dramatic nature of the language of the vachanas. These dialogues are brought together in a dramatic narration of the mission of Allama Prabhu, who is the protagonist of this philosophical drama.

The vachana forms of dialogues are expressed between Prabhu and other contemporary Sharanas. All such encounters turn out to be eye-openers to the Sharanas. Of particular interest are the profound philosophical dialogues between Allama Prabhu and Mukhtayakka, between Allama Prabhu and Siddharama. So is the arrival of Allama and Siddharama in Kalyana and the arrival of Akkamahadevi in Kalyana. Mahadevaiah showed that anthologization could be a creative art. This great achievement in the art of creative anthologization, despite its impressive structuring, is a far cry from the socio-political preoccupations of the twelfth-century movement. At the same time, placing the vachanas in a dialogic situation has recovered the polemical spirit of the Sharana movement. Halage Arya (1500–1530 AD), Gummalapurada Siddhalingayati (circa 1560 AD) and Gulur Siddhavirannarya (circa 1570 AD) produced the later versions.

After the sixteenth century, the vachanas were revived by Tontada Siddhalingayati (circa 1540), whose vachanas are mostly imitative of the twelfth-century vachanas. He lacks the socio-political urgency of his masters. Gummalapurada Siddhalingayati and Svatantra Siddhalingesvara (circa 1560 AD) composed the vachanas by treading the same path as Tontada Siddhalingayati. Ghanalingideva (circa 1700 AD) alone stands out among the later vachanakaras, in spite of the fact that quite a few of his vachanas seem reworkings of twelfth-century masters. His virtue lies in his warmth and poignancy, particularly in the vachanas of devotional love. Kadasiddhesvara (1700–1725 AD) wrote vachanas whose language is deeply influenced by and sometimes mixed with Urdu. Kadakolu Madivalappa (circa

1780 AD), more famous for his swaravachanas, vachanas which could be sung, has also written a highly metaphysical work in the vachana form, *Nijaleelamritada Vachanagalu*. All these attempts at revival show that an old form cannot serve new needs unless new life-blood is infused into it.

Major Shifts in the Literary Context

More than any other event, the twelfth-century flowering of the vachanas, which was itself a by-product of the socio-religious movement of the Virashaiva Sharanas, revolutionized both the idiom and content of Kannada literature. The critical impetus provided by the Sharana movement was revived with different emphases by the Haridasa movement of the sixteenth century. The dominant narrative forms (Kathana) were challenged and altered during this period by the speech/song modes (vachana/pada) as a result of the Sharana revolution in literature. The Sharana socio-religious movement expressed itself mainly through the vachanas. However, the poets of the period also composed numerous compositions called Hadugabbas (sung poems), which are set to a particular raga. This provided the source of inspiration for Vaishnavite Haridasas to develop and enrich song forms like the Kirthane, Suladi and Upabhoga. It should also be remembered that there is a lot of overlap between the vachanas and other song forms. The texts of the vachanas can no doubt be recited like rhythmic prose. However, vachanakaras (Vachana poets) themselves admitted to singing the vachanas. The tradition of singing the vachanas exists in Karnataka to this day. Kannada literature, during the medieval period, moved close to spoken and sung forms and away from the formal nature of early literature as implied by the changeover from the marga (classical) to the desi (folk) mode of poetry.

The emergence of the speech/song genres, instead of supplanting the earlier narrative mode, transformed it into more desi forms. The major narrative works of the period like Harihara's hagiographies of Shaivite saints and the transcreations of the Mahabharata by Kumaravyasa or Lakshmisha are written in the desi metres like the Ragale and the Shatpadi, which lend themselves to song. Since both the Sharana and Haridasa movements sought to reach audiences beyond the narrow circles of the learned, they had to simplify both the diction and syntax of their poetry. Under their influence, the narrative poets also abandoned the use of bombastic words and expressions, involved sentence constructions and artificial conventions like Ashtadas Varnana (eighteen descriptions) that were considered essential to standard works of the previous age. Stereotyped metaphors of poetry were replaced by those taken from everyday life. vachana poets, in particular, strove to get into poetry metaphors taken from all walks of life. This trend had its effect on the great individual geniuses of the period like Harihara, Kumaravyasa and Nanjundakavi.

The overall trend in medieval Kannada literature can be characterized as the vernacularization and popularization of the form and content of poetry. At the same time, however, several poets continued to ape the involved marga traditions. For example, a poet like Shadaksharadeva went on writing Champu poetry as late as the seventeenth century. Such poets do not make up the grandeur of medieval Kannada literature, which is the most productive period, next only to the twentieth century in terms of quality and quantity.

Introduction

Texts

The word 'Sharana' means a person dedicated or committed to Shiva as the supreme godhead. It was one of the several schools of Shaivism. The Sharana movement is considered by one school of thought to constitute the beginning of Virashaivism (heroic Shaivism). The same school considers Basavanna to be the founder of Virashaivism.

It is rare to come across any literary movement elsewhere which produced more than three poets, each with his or her own distinct voice, from all sections of society, high and low, within a period of less than half a century. The fact that this explosion took place in the caste-ridden twelfth-century Karnataka society in which all Shudras, untouchables and women were denied the right to literacy makes the vachana revolution even more amazing. The Sharana movement produced thirty-three women vachana poets, most of them from the lower strata of society. Akkamahadevi, the most famous woman poet of this period, is still the best woman poet of the language. The Sharana movement and the vachanas received great impetus during the lifetime of Basavanna, the great saint poet, who had risen to the high post of finance minister of the Kalachurya emperor, Bijjala, who ruled from Kalyana after usurping the throne from Taila III, the weak Chalukyan ruler. With his profound dedication, commitment and organizational skills, Basavanna was able to attract countless Sharanas to Kalyana. The period of Basavanna's stay in Kalyana coincided with the dramatic events of the Sharana movement and the proliferation of vachana poets.

It is customary for most literary historians and scholars, both conservative and radical, to consider the vachanas to be an expression of the Virashaiva faith. This view is not defensible. Only the works written after the twelfth century, inspired by the vachana movement and with the intention of propagating a well-defined doctrine (the works of Bhimakavi, Chamarasa and others), deserve to be called Virashaiva literature. The significance of the vachanas cannot be found in the propagandist content of some of the more doctrinaire vachana poets like Chennabasavanna or Urilingapeddi. Since the vachanas can be proved to have been composed in the course of discussions and debates in the gatherings of the Sharanas, the basic thrust of the vachanas at their best is one of exploration of spiritual experiences. The brevity and personal urgency of the vachanas imbue them with a kind of intensity rare in marga poetry. Freedom from fixed rules of metre or rhyme enabled the best of the vachana poets to experiment with ever new rhythmic patterns. Though the vachanas do not employ any regular metre or rhyme scheme, their language is marked by internal rhymes and syntactic parallelism. One of the theories about the origin of the vachana is that it originated from the popular metrical form, Tripadi—the three-line stanza. The vachana is meant for the expression of felt intimations rather than the propagation of a well-thought-out religious doctrine. The emphasis on an investigative understanding of spiritual and social realities as well as the rejection of dogmas and superstitions compelled the vachanakaras to challenge, question and debate each other's feelings and ideas. This explanatory nature of the vachanas is not a characteristic feature normally associated with religious literature. It can be argued that the vachanakaras, all of whom were Sharanas, insisted on wearing a Shivalingam on the body, a practice ordained to Virashaivas. Does this not make their composition Virashaiva? True, most vachanakaras

Introduction

attached great importance to the wearing of the Shivalingam. However, vachanakaras themselves often condemned the mere physical act of wearing a Shivalingam. It is also quite probable that vachanakaras like Dakkeya Bommaiah, Nuliya Chandaiah or Gattivalaiah might not have considered the wearing of a Shivalingam as central to being a Sharana. Thus it is better to consider the vachanas a species of collective poetry, consisting of as many distinctive poetic idiolects as the poets themselves. The vachanas were not composed with the intention of producing pure literature but to revolutionize the individual and the society in the light of an innate sense of truth and justice.

While it is true that the Sharana movement had made small beginnings thanks to the missionary activity of a handful of saints, it expanded even before Basavanna's mission in Kalyana began. It is also true that the vachana as a form of poetry survived the twelfth-century socio-religious movement. However, as has already been suggested, it was the active phase of Basavanna's mission that was the highest point in both the Sharana movement and vachana poetry. The Anubhava Mantapa (the Hall of Experience) set up by Basavanna provided a platform for men and women from all sections of society to come together and exchange their perceptions and visions about matters social and spiritual.

Apart from the Sharanas from around Kalyana, many others came in from far-off places after having heard of Basavanna's ever-growing fame. Mendicant Sharanas like Allama Prabhu and Akkamahadevi enriched the Anubhava Mantapa with their presence. The Sharana movement had been critical of caste rules right from the beginning. The Sharanas of Kalyana took the critique of caste rules to its logical conclusion by effecting a scripturally forbidden pratiloma marriage (the marriage between a high-caste girl and a low-caste boy). They married the son of an untouchable Sharana, Haralaiah, to the daughter of a Brahmin Sharana, Madhuvaiah. This audacious violation of scriptures aroused the fury of hegemonic classes who now resolved to put down the Sharana movement. The clash between the conservative ruling class and rebellious Sharanas concluded in most of the Sharanas, including Basavanna, leaving Kalyana and the assassination of the emperor Bijjala. True, vachana poetry survived this gory and disturbing episode. Even in the twentieth century, poets like D.R. Bendre have tried to revive the form. But they could never restore to the form the grandeur and variety of the twelfth century.

To explore the bewildering variety and richness of vachana poetry, we need to acquaint ourselves with the works of some of the most important vachana poets. Basavanna is, of course, the best known of them. The other famous poets of the period are Allama Prabhu, Akkamahadevi, Chennabasavanna and Siddharama. Vachana lore had best be considered an orchestra in which each musician has a distinct contribution to make. While discussing and assessing individual achievements, this point must be kept in mind.

The Earliest Vachanakaras

There are references in the vachanas of Basavanna to earlier Sharanas. The works of at least three such Sharanas have come down to us: Madara Chennaiah, Dohara Kakkaiah and Jedara

Dasimaiah. There is convincing historical evidence to suggest that Madara Chennaiah was the first vachana poet.[4] Unfortunately for us, only ten of his vachanas are now extant. The manner in which this cobbler-saint combines abstract philosophical preoccupations with a vision of a society free from caste and expresses them in concrete metaphors taken from the cobbler's trade is an astounding achievement. Chennaiah set the example of the effective use of metaphors taken from the niceties of one's own profession. This is an example that scores of artisan Sharanas fruitfully emulated in their vachanas. Chennaiah's distrust of caste distinctions also set the tone of the egalitarian commitment of later vachanakaras.

> After erecting three pillars
> The gross, the subtle and the causal bodies.
> After beating the buffaloes' rough hide
> After removing the flesh
> With the staff of the manifest and the hidden
> After tanning the hide with the fibre of dualism
> After pouring the caustic juice of quintessence
> Into the hide-pouch of awareness
> The blemishes of soul thus destroyed
> I have come
> To take the sandals to his feet.
> Take care,
> Not of the ground below,
> But of the path your feet and sandals take.

[4]Shantarasa (ed.), *Modala Vachanakara Madara Chennaiah*, 1983, Shiva Shakti Prakashana, Raichur, pp. 1–9.

> Do not be enslaved
> By the hand-awl, blade or peg
> But realize
> Ramarama, your own true self, the joy of joys!

The details of tanning and making sandals are here converted into metaphors of spiritual transformation. Madara Chennaiah was held in very high esteem in the later Sharana tradition—Basavanna went to the extent of calling him his own father. But Chennaiah is also the father of vachana poetry.

Another untouchable Sharana, Dohara Kakkaiah, is perhaps the second vachanakara. Only six of his vachanas are now available. Unlike Chennaiah who sublimates his caste background, Dohara Kakkaiah appears to be painfully aware of it:

> O, I am doomed.
> I have not touched you even after touching you.
> Cannot my heart touch you even if my hands cannot?

He appears to have pioneered the confessional form of vachanas that figure prominently in Basavanna.

Devara Dasimaiah or Jedara Dasimaiah of the weaver's caste is the only vachanakara of the pre-Basavanna period, a considerable body of whose work is still extant. His existing vachanas number about one hundred and fifty. Several preoccupations of later vachanakaras are already present in Dasimaiah, among them monotheistic faith in Shiva, impatience with convention and cant and a keen sense of actual life situations. Dasimaiah is known for the deft handling of homely metaphors picked from everyday life. The nearness of the rhythm of his vachanas to

Introduction

that of Tripadi gives his vachanas a proverbial ring. He is also a master at embedding idioms and proverbs successfully into his vachanas. Most important of all, brevity is the soul of his vachanas. Dasimaiah was setting the grooves of the anti-royalist attitude of the best of medieval poetry in the following vachana:

> Your gift, the earth;
> Your gift, the harvest;
> Your gift, the wind that blows around;
> People who enjoy your gifts
> And praise others:
> What shall I call such curs?
> O Ramanatha?

Evidently, the poem is a covert attack on court poets of his times. The following vachana is a good example of Dasimaiah's strong grasp of the real, keen powers of observation and indignation against pretentious spirituality:

> He filled a tattered bag with paddy
> And walked all night.
> Afraid of paying toll;
> The paddy was all gone
> Only the bag remained.
> Such is the devotion of the weak-hearted
> O Ramanatha.

Dasimaiah's devotion is based not on fear or guilt, but on courage. When angry with the human condition he challenges god to take on the human form: 'Just once, take on a body, come and see for yourself, You, Ramanatha.' All the major concerns and convictions, forms and idioms of the best of the later vachanakaras exist in Dasimaiah's works. His pious wife, Duggale, was also a poet. It is unfortunate that only two not-so-good vachanas of the first woman-poet of Kannada have survived. Chennaiah and Kakkaiah, the first two dalit poets in Kannada, and Dasimaiah represent a most important strain in Kannada poetry which remains true to its subaltern sources but does not fight shy of metaphysical and spiritual questions.

Basavanna (circa 1150 AD)

With Basavanna, an intensely personal element enters poetry. It is not easy to talk about his work outside the context of his eventful life. His life became the main driving force in a fearless socio-religious struggle against the ossified and inhuman social institutions of caste and gender discrimination; against an economic system supported by the ill-gotten wealth of royal, priestly and mercantile classes; against the perpetual dehumanizing slavery of the majority, the labouring castes and untouchables; against institutionalized, temple-centred spirituality accessible only to the privileged handful; against learning devoid of compassion and ignorance steeped in superstition. As a poet, Basavanna fought against all those rules and conventions that suffocated the irrepressible force of what one saw and felt. This is most powerfully expressed in the following vachana:

> Never heard
> Of tunes and rhythms
> Or keeping count of cymbal beats.

Introduction

> Nor about feet
> Ambrosial or divine.
> O master Kudalasangama
> As no harm can ever come to you
> I sing as I please.

More facts are known about Basavanna's life than about any other twelfth-century Sharana. Born into an orthodox Shaivite Brahmin family in Bagewadi, he became disillusioned with the blind and bigoted conventions of his surroundings at a very young age. He left home in search of a refuge and found it in Kudalasangama, at the confluence of two rivers. An enlightened sage, Jatavedamuni, headed a very famous institution of learning located there. From him, Basavanna must have learnt the scriptures and sciences of the day. At the same time he developed a profound devotion to Kudalasangama, a form of Shiva and the deity of the temple at the confluence. Later, as a young man, he went to Mangalavede, the then capital of Bijjala; the Kalachurya king and feudatory to Taila III, the Chalukyan emperor ruling from Kalyana. Basavanna took a clerical job at Mangalavede and his efficiency not only brought him fame but also got him recognition of the king.

In Mangalavede, Basavanna probably married two wives, Gangambike and Nilambike. Bijjala succeeded in overthrowing and usurping the throne of the emperor by taking advantage of the political unrest in the empire. After becoming emperor, he elevated Basavanna to the high post of finance minister. Basavanna moved to Kalyana with his two devout wives, his pious sister, Akka Nagamma, and his nephew, Chennabasavanna. With the active co-operation of these dedicated family members, he started working towards building a spiritual home for all Sharanas which was to become the centre for the dissemination of the teachings of the Sharanas. His house came to be called Mahamane (Great House). He also set up the Anubhava Mantapa where Sharanas of all classes and castes gathered. All of them engaged in learned interactions with each other. They criticized, questioned, challenged, corrected, confirmed or corroborated each other's views. Their path of devotion was not based on abject acceptance. Their attack on superstitious practices was uncompromising. First-hand experience alone became the test of spiritual height and human dignity. Basavanna's fame spread far and wide and spiritual seekers and adepts poured into Kalyana. Privileged institutions like the Agraharas and temples could not be mute spectators any more.

The Sharana movement had raised the morale of the artisan castes. They had become not just literate but literary figures. Cobblers and town criers, street performers and prostitutes, washermen and potters, cowherds and tavern keepers—all such new converts to the Sharana movement had become spiritually awakened, politically conscious and socially aware. Most of them made learned attacks on the foundations of the existing order. Another slap in the face of caste society was the unprecedented marriage that Sharanas effected between an untouchable boy and a Brahmin girl. The priestly and merchant classes were shocked and the emperor was forced to take the side of conservatives. In this tense atmosphere, Basavanna was divested of his office and perhaps expelled from the capital. And then came the storm. The conflict between the Sharanas and the ruling class turned violent. Those involved in the sacrilegious marriage were blinded and sentenced to death,

Introduction

which, in turn, led to the assassination of Bijjala. The privileged sections unleashed terror on the Sharanas, some of whom fought their way out of Kalyana and sought refuge in Ulavi. Basavanna met his end in Kudalasangama, probably around this time. The Sharana movement was put down and most Sharanas left Kalyana for different destinations. The most glorious age in the literary and social history of Karnataka had come to an end. Later attempts at reviving the movement could not recover the lost glory.

Basavanna was the leading, if not the only, actor in this exciting drama. The aspirations and ideals, the tensions and trials of the epoch are echoed in his vachanas. He was not just a saint, but also a man of the world. He was sensitive to the subtle nuances of the word and idiom. His world of metaphors is, therefore, all inclusive. Sometimes tranquil, sometimes stormy, but always imbued with deep devotion all the time, his vachanas cover the whole gamut of human experiences and emotions. He has been compared to Kalidasa because of his gift for metaphors.[5] But the comparison is only a half truth as Basavanna's metaphors show a much greater diversity. There are other poets of the period who are more intense, more profound and more socially aware than him but none of them had his many-faceted understanding, which perhaps has made him one of the best-loved poets of the language despite the fact that his poetry was a by-product of his spiritual and social mission.

By the deeply personal element of his poetry is meant not an inordinate interest in autobiography or obsession with one's

---

[5] M.R. Srinivasamurthy, *Vachanadharmasara*, 1977, Mysore University, Mysore, p. 189.

Introduction

own egoistic designs. It is the warmth, the intimacy, the feel, born of a total but conscious involvement in one's own values. Basavanna's confessional vachanas are often deeply moving. No Kannada poet has ever been so self-critical as Basavanna. The discovery of the minutest defect in himself frightens him into a plaintive cry:

> Like the dog on the palanquin,
> This heart
> Does not give up the old ways
> The moment it sees you know what
> It goes back to its old ways.
> O burn, burn this heart.
> That runs towards sensual things
> But does not let me remember.
>
> Day after day, you, O Master
> O my master Kudalasangama
> Be so kind that I may remember
> Your feet—I beg, I pray

Many are the occasions on which he complains when confronted with the harsh world of senses: 'Father, father, listen to my yelling.' It is the unbearable harshness of the mundane world that pushes him into the arms of Shiva:

> I am just one person
> But there are five of them
> Burning me.

Introduction

> When a tiger is dragging
> The wild bull away,
> Can you not rescue it
> O master Kudalasangama?

Basavanna's social criticism is as merciless as his self-criticism. This is reflected in the following vachana:

> What if you go riding the elephant?
> What if you go riding the horse?
> What if you go wearing
> Vermilion and kasturi scent
> O Brother?
> O you have gone without realizing
> The essence of truth
> O you have gone without sowing or reaping
> The yield of virtue
> O riding the inebriated elephant of pride
> You have become destiny's target
> O without seeing our lord
> Kudalasangama
> You have become a target for hell.

His criticism of hypocrites and impostors of every kind is expressed in some of the best satirical poems in the language. In one such poem he depicts a snake-charmer and his wife on their way to find a bride for their son, cancelling their journey the moment they see a bad omen—another snake charmer and his wife. His oft-quoted didactic poems are extremely popular. They convince us not by forcing belief on us, but by winning our hearts even before we know it.

A brief survey like this can at best give a very faint idea of the masterful use of the word, image and rhythm in Basavanna's vachanas. They still remain a source of joy, comfort and illumination for the learned and the laity. But it is the encyclopaedic breadth of the worlds that go into Basavanna's vachanas that have earned him pride of place among Kannada poets.

Akkamahadevi (circa 1150 AD)

The epic range of Basavanna's vachanas can be contrasted with the lyrical depth of Akkamahadevi's vachanas. In her poetry, the personal intensity is indistinguishable from the luminosity of mysticism. Born into a merchant family in Uduthadi, she grew up into a maiden of great beauty, which intoxicated the local king, Kaushika. Whether or not this devotional-minded girl married Kaushika is a point about which her later hagiographers differ. There is ample evidence, though indirect, in her vachanas that she was forced into this marriage. No wonder it soon broke down. She walked out of the palace through the streets of the town into a vast and hostile world in search of her divine beloved and husband, Channamallikarjuna, the lord of fragrant jasmines. She had to pass savage tests in the man's world; she had to brave hunger, thirst and dangers. At last an enlightened sage, she entered the city of Kalyana and reached Basavanna's spiritual home. Even the Sharanas gave her a difficult time, asking her many questions. But she took the challenge, gave them satisfactory answers and won the admiration and respect of all Sharanas including that of Allama Prabhu, the most fastidious one. She is said to have attained final samadhi in Kadali, the dense forest in the Srisaila mountains, now in Andhra Pradesh. This is broadly her life story told by her hagiographers. But her inner story that unfolds itself through her three hundred odd available vachanas is much more dramatic. They express the different moods, feelings, experiences and situations that go to make up one single theme: 'the joy of being at one with Channamallikarjuna after having parted.' Her language is imbued with the poignant tone of someone intoxicated with divine love. Her poetry compares well with those of other women saint poets like Lalleswari, Meera and Andal. Her metaphors are mostly from nature, which she sees as pervaded by Channamallikarjuna:

> You are the whole forest
> You are all the divine trees in the forest
> You are all the birds and beasts
> Sporting amidst trees
> O Channamallikarjuna,
> Though all is filled with you
> Why don't you show me your face
> Turned away from me?

In her quest for the unseen face of the beloved she came upon many obstacles, some of which were posed by men blind with lust. This is how she tries to expostulate with someone attracted by her body—'a pit of shit, a pot of piss, a trap of bones and stinking pus,' according to her:

> Don't hold me. Don't
> Stop me. Let go
> Of my hand, the hem

Introduction

> Of my sari. Don't
> You know of the worst hell
> For those that break
> The promise made in black and white?
> You shall be doomed
> If you touch the woman
> Married to Channamallikarjuna.

She was the first devotional poet to see maya in a man's form and not just in women. A group of her vachanas captures the ecstasy of being married to 'the deathless, defectless, formless and handsome one':

> Guru became kin,
> Linga, the bridegroom
> And I, the bride.
> The whole world knows
> That countless devotees are my parents
> Who gave me in marriage
> Finding the ideal groom
> Channamallikarjuna is my husband,
> O Brother,
> No one else can be my man.

Apart from the vachanas, Akkamahadevi has written the *Yoganga Trividhi* which describes different phases of spiritual enlightenment in cryptic language. Like the other Sharanas, she has composed a small number of songs of which the most famous is entitled *O Ferryman, I trust you.*

Introduction

Allama Prabhu (circa 1150 AD)

If Basavanna is the most lovable and Akkamahadevi the most fascinating of vachana poets, Allama is the most cryptic. Not always does he speak a forbidding language, though. At times, he can be as refreshingly simple as in the following vachana:

> Sunrise, is it?
> Sundown, over?
> Ah, they have vanished,
> All formations made of water
> Darkness caved
> In all the three worlds
> Tell me
> What is the enigma
> Of all this, O Gogeshwara?

But even such simplicity is only apparent. At the highest reaches of mysticism in poetry, Allama's vachanas time and again point to the inadequacy of language: 'Alas, look at the coyness of the word' and comparisons of all kinds: 'When you become the origin of light, what similes shall I find?' However, 'A man who knows himself can speak and at the same time, manage not to be contaminated by speech,' says Allama Prabhu to Muktayakka, a fellow mystic; he therefore uses language against language, symbols against symbols, resulting in the curious situation of the word turning back on itself, devouring itself, so one is face to face with 'just that' (tanu), which is beyond 'I' (nanu) or 'you' (neenu). He resorts to a language of paradoxes and inversions, to the bedagu mode.

Introduction

All poetic and legendary accounts of Allama's life are either allegorical or hyperbolic. Nevertheless, Harihara, the first poetic hagiographer gives a few hints. Allama, born in the caste of temple-performers in Balligave, now in the Shimoga district, grew up into a handsome youth, expert in playing maddale, a special kind of drum. While performing at a temple, he fell in love with the temple dancer, Kamalathe. She reciprocated instantly. They drank deep the bliss of conjugal love. But the unexpected happened. A fatal illness took her away. Like all legendary lovers, Allama went insane. This lasted until he discovered a garden, a hidden temple where Animisha his guru awaited. Initiated into the secrets of the Linga, Allama became enlightened. From then a Yogi of Yogis, he went about awakening the partially awakened Sharanas to 'just that'. His vachanas seem composed mostly during his life as a Jangama, which means, among other things, a holy mendicant. The acceptance of Allama's spiritual authority and authenticity was almost universal in the community of Sharanas; they urged him to head the Anubhava Mantapa. Allama later became one with the Linga (lingaikya) in Kadali.

Most devotional and mystical poets are caught up in names and forms. Allama is always looking beyond. He thus comes down hard on those holding on to symbols as in the following vachana:

> Darkness, the grasping hand, O Friend
> Darkness, the seeing eye, O Friend
> Darkness, the remembering heart, O Friend.
> All darkness, two-headed, on this side, O Friend.
> Gogeshwara's form,
> His face turned away
> Is on the other side, O Friend.

Introduction

His attack on systems, customs and practices, including those of the Sharanas, can be extremely harsh. But they spring not from sectarian, or even social concerns, but from purely spiritual ones. Contrast, for instance, Allama's rejection of temples with Basavanna's famous vachana, 'The rich build temples for Shiva.'

> I saw
> The fragrance fleeing
> When the bee came.
> I saw
> Intellect fleeing
> When the heart came.
> I saw
> The temple fleeing
> When God came,
> O Gogeshwara!

Here is an example of Allama's tough bedagu mode:

> The deer with the tiger's head
> The tiger with the deer's head
> The two—joined at the waist—
> It is not the tiger, not the deer
> But something else
> Come to eat next. Look!
> When the body without the head
> Grazes—

Introduction

> Look, O Gogeshwara,
> The leaf vanishes.

It is such vachanas, hard but shining like diamonds, that inspired a whole tradition of exegesis in the following centuries. The blinding clarity found in Allama's impassioned utterances is unparalleled in vachana poetry or elsewhere. If Basavanna's images are rooted in society and Akkamahadevi's in nature, Allama's images stem from a deeper, archetypal source. This can be clearly seen in the following vachana:

> The earth and the sky are
> Stomached in a living thing
> Tell me,
> What is great here
> To him that does not call it great?
> Tell me,
> What is trivial here
> To him that does not call it trivial?
> If greatness enters the heart
> Is there anything like it
> O Gogeshwara?

A feeling of wonder runs through Allama's works. His meanings always elude us but his images haunt us. Like Koans, the riddles used in the Japanese Zen tradition, Allama's vachanas shock us out of complacency and send us looking for 'our faces before we were born'. Beyond man-made languages, images and abstractions, Allama's works stand in a dazzling brilliance, the 'rising of a hundred million suns'.

Chennabasavanna (circa 1150 AD)

The nephew and a close associate of Basavanna, Chennabasavanna played an important role in the management of Basavanna's Mahamane. His contemporaries often mention his prodigious learning admiringly. Quite a few of his vachanas are longer than usual and he was a prolific writer. Apart from vachanas, *Mantragopya*, a mystical work describing phases of a Yogi's experience, is attributed to him. However, the poetic value of his vachanas is not very high. He was essentially a thinker and a theologian, interested in minute classification and elaborate system building. He perhaps pointed the way to the systematic theological and exegetical works of Virashaivism of the later period. However, once in a while he can write vachanas as telling as Basavanna's:

> They measure the heap
> Of a life
> With huge jars of
> The sunrise and the sunset.
> Before the heap is emptied
> Give up
> The false shows of pleasures.
> Offer
> Worship to Shivalinga
> Whoever does not
> Goes to the worst hell.

Introduction

Siddharama (circa 1150 AD)

Siddharama is yet another prolific vachana poet and an influential Sharana. He was born in Sonnalagi—now Sholapur in Maharashtra—where he spent most of his life. His philosophy was one of service to mankind, the path of Karmayoga. Allama Prabhu taught him to grow out of this and the two went to Kalyana together. Siddharama was deeply rewarded by the interactions with the Sharanas of the Anubhava Mantapa. He later returned to his hometown.

Siddharama claims to have written sixty-eight thousand vachanas out of which only 1,379 are extant. He shares the worldview of other vachana poets in his rejection of blind conventions and caste and gender discrimination and emphasizes on realization through personal experience. He shows a deep influence of Basavanna's vachanas. He too borrows metaphors from diverse spheres of everyday life. Apart from vachanas he has written several devotional works in Tripadi.

Siddharama is at his best when he charges a quotidian event with far-reaching significance:

> A cock crows
> Day in, day out
> O they do not heed,
> The multitudes of dying men
> If you know
> No birth, no bondage for you.
> If you do not,
> No end to your births and deaths
> O Kapilasiddhamallikarjuna.

Other Vachana Poets

A large number of other vachana poets came from the class of artisans. Quite a few of them belonged to castes whose professions were looked down upon in the caste hierarchy. The beginning of the Sharana movement was not imposed from above but was born from below as a result of cooperation between Jangamas like Revanasiddha (a shepherd by caste) and Marulasiddha (an untouchable by caste) and spiritually minded artisans like Madara Chennaiah and Devara Dasimaiah. Thus the very roots of the Sharana movement were in the rejection of caste-based inequality. Basavanna opened wide the doors of his Great House for all castes. As a consequence, there was a boom in vachana writing among the lower strata: Molige Maraiah (a woodcutter), Madivala Machideva (a washerman), Ambigara Chowdaiah (a ferryman), Vaidya Sanganna (a doctor), Madara Dhoolaiah (a cobbler), Hendada Maraiah (a toddy-tapper), Turugahi Ramanna (a cowherd), Aydakki Maraiah (a rice gatherer), Medara Ketaiah (a basket-maker), Nuliya Chandaiah (a rope-maker), Kannadi Kayakada Remmitande (a barber), Vokkaliga Muddanna (a farmer), Muktinathaiah (a town-crier). These give us an idea of the variety of caste backgrounds of the vachanakaras. A burglar by profession, Kannada Maritande also turned into a Sharana and wrote vachanas. These poets are by no means passive followers of any leader. Most of them do look up to the luminaries of the movement like Basavanna and Allama, but there are occasions when they criticize even their leaders fearlessly, as found, for instance, in some vachanas of Madivala Machideva. They also attack false and hypocritical Jangamas in harsh terms. Their opposition to caste discrimination is based not on the feeling of upper-caste guilt like in Basavanna, but on the anger and shame of the humiliated. A large number of these poets carry on the tradition of Madara Chennaiah and use metaphors taken from their own professions. This poetic practice is an offshoot of their commitment to the philosophy of Kayaka (the dignity of labour), which seems to be the contribution of Sharanas from the lower strata. Some of them, like Madivala Machideva and Hadapada Appanna, played decisive roles during the upheaval in Kalyana and defended the interest of the Sharanas bravely. Each one of these artisan poets has worked out his own distinct idiom. Here is Machideva's attack on false vachanakaras:

> The vain entertainers
> Who speak strings of vachanas
> Are they devotees, O Friend?
> Vachanas are not like them
> Neither are they like vachanas.
> The reason is this—
> At their back
> Only the concerns of flesh and fortune
> In front of them
> Just a haystack of words.
> Like a dog wagging its tail
> When he sees his master,
> Their words.
> O father Kalidevaradeva.

Ambigara Chowdaiah, the most furious of the vachanakaras, could also be deeply serene at moments:

Introduction

> Here I come, a ferryman without a body
> To the great flowing river
> If you pay the price—
> Your mind
> That grasps and lets go,
> I shall take you across
> The great stream
> To the end,
> To the village
> Without words or limits,
> Says Chowdaiah the ferryman.

Sometimes, their involvement in labour is so deep that they consider it superior even to Shiva. Thus Madara Dhoolaiah bids Shiva leave when he appears when Dhoolaiah is making sandals: 'Why do you come here to the one carrying this bag of flesh? Go, go back to your silver mountain, the haunt of your devotees.'

There was a group of vachanakaras that belonged to the class of beggars and street performers. The best known of these are Dakkeya Bommaiah, Bahuroopi Chowdaiah, Kalaketaiah and Nageya Maritande. These also employ the imagery of their trades. Unlike most Sharanas, Dakeya Bommaiah continued to worship Mari but transcended it through the essential philosophy of the Sharanas. His profession was to go begging, carrying the idol of Mari on his head, and beating a drum called the Dakke. Says Bommaiah: 'Before the beats of the Dakke cease, know Bhimeswara, the destroyer of time.'

Some poets of this class resort to the cryptic mode of bedagu, the chief among them being Hadapada Appanna (of the barber caste) and vachana Bhandari Shantarasa. Manumuni Gummatadeva, a former Jaina, and Gupta Manchanna, a former Vaishnava, try in their vachanas to realize the faith of the Sharanas through the symbols of their old faiths and stand out for their reason. Gajesha Masanaiah and Urilingadeva have written beautiful lyrics of spiritual love assuming women's personae. The identification with Sharanasati (Sharana bride) is so complete that it is hard to believe that their vachanas were written by men. At times they attain the same intensity as Akkamahadevi. As an example, consider the following vachana of Gajesha Masanaiah:

> When I saw him
> I forgot the eight directions, O Mother.
> O Mother, Mother
> When I got him to speak to me
> My entire body broke into sweat
> What next, O Mother?
> Today when Mahalinga Gajeshwara
> Is embracing me
> I have forgotten
> To embrace him ...
> What next, O Mother?

Adaiah, who has written a huge body of vachanas, and Urilingapeddi continue with the theological strain represented by Chennabasavanna.

In summary, the involvement in the Sharana movement of saint poets from different caste backgrounds stretched the boundaries of the metaphor to the excluded areas of experience and produced the first expressions of rebellious poetry, which is unsurpassed till now for its variety and vigour.

Women Vachana Poets

Apart from Akkamahadevi's, the vachanas composed by thirty-three Sharanes (feminine of Sharanas) are extant. Just as the emphasis on Basavanna and Allama often marginalizes the achievement of other vachanakaras, the emphasis on Akkamahadevi's vachanas is placed to the exclusion of other women poets of the period. Three leading women vachana poets are Basavanna's wives, Gangambike and Nilambike, and his elder sister, Nagalambike. All the three were actively involved in Basavanna's mission. Their vachanas give many interesting hints about Basavanna, whom they had seen closely. They have all written vachanas extolling Basavanna's virtues. The vachanas of Nilambike are available in a larger number than those of the other two. Here is a very elusive kind of metaphysical poetry that captures different facets of a spiritual marriage. It does not have the tenderness of Akkamahadevi's vachanas but an elusive beauty all its own. She has composed a handful of elegant vachanas following Basavanna's passing away such as:

> Long ago an infant was born.
> A ruby placed in its hands
> Appeared, in many colours
> And then took refuge

Introduction

> In emptiness,
> For Basava
> Whose name is lost in Sangaiah.

Quite a few women poets were the wives of male vachanakaras. Duggale, the wife of Dasimaiah, has already been referred to. Other women poets are Lakkamma, the wife of Aydakki Maraiah, the wife of Urilingapeddi, Ketaladevi, the wife of Gundaiah, Guddavve, the wife of Bachi Basavaiah, the comb-maker, Mahadevi, the wife of Molige Maraiah, Lingamma, the wife of Hadapada Appanna and so on. Mahadevi and Lingamma often write from a lofty spiritual viewpoint about subtleties of mystical experience. Lingamma speaks a cryptic but haunting language:

> The mind grows dull
> The body vanishes
> The breath stops
> The flame appears
> The smoke spreads
> The lake is all burnt down.
> Unless you go in,
> Open the door
> And immerse yourself in light
> There is no true freedom,
> Said Chennabasavanna, dear to Appanna.

Kalavve, the first dalit woman poet, vent her fury against the hypocrisy of high castes and religious men. She asks:

Introduction

> They say—
> All those are high born
> Who eat sheep, fowl and tiny fish,
> They say—
> All those are low born
> Who eat the cow that rains on Shiva
> Sacred milk sanctified five times.
> What the Brahmins had eaten adorned the grass
> And a dog licked it up and went away.
> What the cobblers had eaten adorned the grass—
> Now Brahmins' ornament.
> In other words
> Bags are made of cow's hide
> For ghee and for water.
> Senseless Brahmins who drink
> Ghee and water from such leather bags
> Thinking it sacred
> They can't escape
> Utmost perdition.
> The master of Urilingapeddi
> Doesn't approve of such men.

Amuge Rayamma and Akkamma share Kalavve's indignation against religious charlatans. Their satirical vachanas are as powerful as those of Ambigara Chowdaiah. Kadire Remmavve, of the spinner caste, is an interesting poet employing the cryptic bedagu mode effectively. Muktayakka, whom Allama Prabhu engaged in a profound debate, and Bonthadevi, a princess, explore aspects of spiritual experience in an oblique language. Writes Bonthadevi:

> The emptiness in the body
> The emptiness in the monastery
> Empty, empty, emptiness ...
> Emptiness, the whole of one's self
> O emptiness, carefree!

Satyakka is another poet who at times attained the same heights of mystical love as Akkamahadevi.

On the whole, the achievement of women poets of the period is as impressive in quality as that of men poets in spite of the fact that the quantity of their output now extant is less.

Vachanas in the Bedagu Mode

The stream of bedagu among the vachanas belongs to the same species of verbal structures as riddles in folklore. Riddles attempt to 'find directions through indirections out'. In our folklore, riddles state something indirectly, which needs to be deciphered into simple terms by the listener. It is an exercise to the listener's powers of problem solving. Vachanakaras use this form of communication popular with common folk, for mystical experience is not communicable in straightforward language. Allama Prabhu has written the best vachanas in this mode. The others who have excelled in this include most of the vachana poets from artisan classes.

A bedagina vachana speaks through paradoxes and inversions. It aims to shock the reader out of his conventional way of seeing and feeling. It has also been likened to the tradition of sandhya bhasa (twilight language) used in Tantrik traditions both to communicate and conceal higher truths. Bedagina vachana sometimes resorts to conventional symbolism or numerical symbolism. Hence it has been suggested that these vachanas be read only in the light of traditional commentaries.[6] This does not appear to be easy as not all bedagina vachanas employ traditional symbolism. In particular, such compositions by artisan poets draw upon images from their own profession. From the thirteenth century onwards, elaborate commentaries came to be written of bedagina vachanas, the most important of them being the one by Singalada Siddhabasava (circa 1600 AD), who attempts to reduce the import of the vachanas to the concepts of latter-day Virashaiva theology. In the recent days, scholars are trying to offer readings of bedagina vachanas in non-theological terms.[7] Here is an example of a bedagina vachana employing conventional symbolism:

> You who tasted the milk
> From three breasts
> Saw ten states
> Tell me: Who are you?
> It's a pity you came
> To the undivided town
> To suffer pain
> Your past, forgotten,
> Now a victim of doubt.
> Know the gap between the two states—
> Your own self, O Bheemeshwaralinga.

[6]M. Chidanandamurthy, *Vachana Sahitya,* 1971, Bangalore University, Bangalore, p. 81.
[7]For a discussion of this subject from new angles, see Baragoor Ramachandrappa (ed.), *Bedagina Vachana Parampare,* 1994, Karnataka Sahitya Academy, Bangalore.

> O bodiless companion
> Burning of the forest of good deeds.

In this vachana, the numbers used—three, ten and two—are traditional symbols in esoteric mystical schools. Three breasts mean three bodies; ten means senses, five jnandriyas and five karmendriyas; two, the polarity of the soul and god. However, note that the following vachana by Ramanna, the cowherd, uses only images from the world of commonsense and his profession:

> At dawn,
> I keep vigil of Brahma.
> At noon
> I keep vigil of Vishnu
> At sunset
> I keep vigil of Rudra
> After dark
> After driving the herd
> Back to their folds …
> O when shall I be rid of this cowherd's staff?
> No,
> This cowherd's staff shall not drop
> From my hands
> Until Vishveshwaralinga, the lord of cattle,
> Ceases to be.

Swaravachanas: Musical Compositions

Though vachanas are understood as a form of prose poetry, it should be kept in mind that they can be sung. However, they are not composed to suit a specific raga or tala. They can therefore be read, recited or even performed (as some performing Sharanas like Bahuroopi Chowdaiah would). Sharanas have also written musical compositions called Swaravachanas, which provided models for the musical compositions of the Haridasas later. The suggestion has also been made that both vachanas and swaravachanas are two types of musical compositions.

All the leading vachanakaras have written swaravachanas that resemble, in thought and imagery, their non-musical compositions. Swaravachanas are written in a more formal diction than vachanas to meet the needs of another art—music. On the whole, there is a greater element of the esoteric bedagu mode in musical vachanas than in the other type. Further, they have more of theological content.

Nevertheless, a handful of swaravachanas, particularly those by Akkamahadevi and Allama, are as effective as their vachanas. Here is a sample from Allama:

> O Lord, my Lord, protect me.
> O Lord, my Lord,
> Let my mother-in-law's eyes be pierced
> Let death break my brother-in-law's legs
> Let the wall in the backyard give way
> And dense darkness come and engulf it
> Let the he-man of the house disappear
> And the useless brother-in-law go mad
> Let the sister-in-law here die
> And go to the world of the sun
> Let the baby's eyes be shut.

Introduction

> Let the moon by bitten by a snake
> Today let Lord Gogeswaralinga
> Come and be one with me.[8]

Another view of such songs is that they were not originally composed by twelfth-century Sharanas themselves, but by their followers who turned prose poems into musical compositions.

Theological Context

It is clear that the composition of the vachanas took place as part of a collective socio-religious movement that mounted a fierce attack on orthodox values. It would, however, be hasty to conclude that the vachanakaras were merely an unorthodox group with anti-Brahmanical leanings. Their criticisms of other schools of philosophy were equally severe. Not even other schools of Shaivism, which also believed in the supremacy of Shiva, were spared. Neither were the followers of other faiths like Vaishnavism, Natha Siddha cults and Tantra. Attacks were also directed against popular superstitions.[9] The period of the vachanakaras was characterized by intense inter-faith conflicts and debates. We not only find vachanakaras criticizing the viewpoints of others but also evolving a philosophy that embodies their own values. This philosophical impulse is not shared by all vachanakaras in equal measure. Chennabasavanna was the poet in whose compositions the tendency towards philosophical and doctrinal systematization

---

[8] L. Basavaraju (ed.), *Shivadasa Gitanjali*, Second edition, 1990, Mysore, p. 251.

[9] A.K. Ramanujan, introduction to *Speaking of Siva*, 1973, Penguin Books, Baltimore, p. 23.

figures most prominently. At the other end of the pole is Allama, whose grasp of spirituality is so intensely personal and experimental that quite often his compositions take on overtones of anarchism, as for instance, in the following vachana:

> Eating from the skull, playing in graveyards
> That's his anti-normal nature.
> Hard, hard to penetrate, this expert
> Gogeshwara alone is an outcaste
> Polluted, all the rest.

However, most of the poets in question have composed both experiential and doctrinal vachanas. The proportion between the two types of composition varies from poet to poet. Before we proceed to examine the complex inter-relationships between the doctrinal and experiential dimensions of the vachanas, it is necessary to take a brief look at the fundamental tenets that are normally associated with the faith of the vachanakaras.

vachana lore is usually considered to be the expression of Virashaivism or Lingayatism, a branch of Shaivism. According to some, Basavanna, the key figure of the vachana movement, is the founder of this new branch of Shaivism.[10] According to others, it is not so. Virashaivism, they argue, is an ancient faith whose roots are traceable to the most ancient Agamic tradition.[11] Attempts have also been made by some scholars to establish continuity

---

[10] This is the conclusion arrived at by M.R. Sakhre, *History and Philosophy of Lingayat Religion*, 1978, Karnataka University, Dharwar.

[11] Characteristic of this view are the arguments advanced in S.C. Nandimath, *A Handbook of Veerashaivism*, 1941, Literary Committee, L.E. Association, Dharwar.

Introduction

between the Vedas and the tenets of Virashaivism. Nijaguna Shivayogi, a fifteenth-century saint poet, has laboured long and hard in his prolific writings to reconcile Vedism and Virashaivism. The first-hand reading of the incredibly voluminous vachana corpus suggests that vachana texts, though mostly individual experience-oriented and anti-Brahmanical in spirit, bear such a highly complex relationship to other schools that most of the above arguments seem partial and selective.[12]

Like other schools of Shaivism, Virashaivism also believes in the supremacy of Shiva. But Virashaiva monotheism, as expressed in the sayings of some of its chief spokesmen like Basavanna and Chennabasavanna, is much more exclusive and militant than in other schools of Shaivism—Pratyabhijna, Spanda or Tryambaka schools of Kashmir Shaivism, for instance.[13] Unlike the Shaiva Siddhanta school of Tamil Nadu, Virashaivism attaches little importance to Shiva worship expressed in temple rituals.[14] However, the daily chanting of the vedic rudra-prasna accompanied by abhisheka is widely practised in several Virashaiva shrines and mutts today. The Virashiavas of the twelfth century rejected temples because temples in those days were confined

---

[12]Blake R. Michael, *The Origins of Virashaiva Sects*, 1992, Motilal Banarsidass, Delhi, p. 9. He holds that Virashaivism is essentially in consonance with Brahmanism. K.G. Nagarajappa advances cogent arguments that Virashaivism brought no radical change in the lives of the underprivileged castes. See *Maruchintane*, 1985, Pranathi Prakashana, Tumkur.

[13]These schools see Shiva more as a cosmic principle than as a deity whereas in Vachana lore, there is ambiguity on this subject. For an account of these schools, refer to Mark S.G. Dykczkowski, *The Stanzas on Vibration*, 1994, Dilipkumar Publishers, Varanasi.

[14]Indira Viswanathan Peterson, *Poems to Siva: The Hymns of the Tamil Saints*, 1991, Motilal Banarsidass, Delhi, p. 11.

to upper castes and classes. Shiva is worshipped by virashaivas in the form of the Linga worn on the body in a tiny casket known of the karadige. It is to be conferred on the Virashaiva after due initiatory rites by a qualified guru and is called the Istalinga, as opposed to Sthavara Lingas (fixed Lingas) of temples. Most of the Sharanas have underlined the wearing of Istalinga. Whoever wears the Linga in this way and follows the Virashaiva tenets is, in theory, admitted into the faith as an equal among believers. He becomes a Bhakta (a Virashaiva follower) as opposed to a Bhavi (a non-Virashaiva outsider).

Like all mystics, vachanakaras often doubt the capability of words and concepts to express the unitive experience of truth. Says Allama of the unitive experience of truth: 'Look, look at the coyness of words.' It is precisely on this ground that Muktayakka objects to Allama's chatter when he opens the discussion with her on spiritual matters in *Shoonya Sampadane*. Allama's reply to her is: 'All language is the essence of beyond if one knows oneself. All language is ignorance if one is unaware of oneself.'[15] This explains why vachanakaras, who often denounce scriptures as 'a haystack of words', an expression used by Ambigara Chowdaiah, compare vachanas by enlightened saints to Parusha, the philosopher's stone. 'Vachana, though speech, is beyond speech,' says Siddharama.

Vachanas can be viewed as the expression in words of the unitive participation with the Divine (Anubhava) on the part of the Sharanas. At the same time, a theological system was developed to explain the same experience conceptually. One is

---

[15] S.C. Nandimath *et. al.* (eds.), *Shoonya Sampadane*, Vol. 1, 1965, Karnataka University, Dharwar, pp. 126–205.

the expression, the other, explanation. One works with feelings, the other with reason. It is for this reason that the vachanas have a deeper and wider appeal than Virashaiva theology, which is of interest only to the serious-minded votaries of a particular faith. Virashaiva theology, however, needs to be introduced briefly here for two reasons. Firstly, though vachanas at their best approximate the ideal of transcending the expressible, they were composed in the polemical context of their times, when their spokesmen were engaged in contests and competition with followers of other faiths to demonstrate the superiority of their own faith. Further, the vachanas sometimes directly illustrate theological concepts and propositions. Though such illustrations are mostly in a dry and unpoetic language, there are times when it is not so. Here, for example, is a vachana by Basavanna:

> The lake's ornament, the naidile flower;
> The sea's ornament, the wave;
> The sky's ornament, the moon;
> Woman's ornament, her virtue;
> The ornament of Kudalasangama's devotees,
> The vibhuti on their forehead.

The vachana is a justification of vibhuti, one of the eight sheaths mandatory for a Virashaiva. Three successive metaphors have a beauty of their own. This is an example of how poetry is sometimes found alongside theology in the vachanas. Though it is possible to distinguish the poetic from the theological vachanas, the two are not mutually exclusive. Apart from composing direct illustrations of theological ideas, vachanakaras have also composed theological vachanas. Chennabasavanna's *Karana*

Hasige, Allama's *Mantragopya* and Akkamahadevi's *Yoganga Trividhi* are works of this nature.

Secondly, yet another way of employing the theological scheme of Shatsthala is possible. The dialogic nature of the vachanas has been hinted at earlier. Most often the vachanas, when read individually, appear as pieces of a dialogue cut out of a dramatic or a narrative context. The inbuilt dramatic feature of the vachana texts are complemented by the narrative scheme provided by the Shatsthala system in terms of the individual's progress from the plane of diversity to the plane of unitive experience. Later editors of the vachanas read this scheme into the texts and this is expressed in their arrangement of the vachanas. The anthologies of *Shoonya Sampadane* deviated from this scheme in stringing the vachanas together along the narrative thread of the life of Allama. A fairly large number of twentieth century collections and anthologies have adhered to the Shatsthala-based arrangement of the vachanas and have incorporated the sub-phases of the system worked out by vachana scholars of the age of compilation from the fifteenth century onwards.

One can suggest another way of relating this scheme to the vachanas. Just as the European sonnet sequences tell a story running through all the sonnets put together, the vachanas can be seen as a sequence from which a unifying story can be read. This is the story of a (wo)man's journey from the bondage of divided existence to the liberation of unitive participation in the divine. Some vachanakaras like Basavanna, Akkamahadevi, Gajesha Masanaiah and Urilingadeva narrate this journey in terms of a love story between the human bride and the divine bridegroom. Others like Allama employ more abstract types

Introduction

of storytelling. This story is common to most of the female vachana poets except to a few like Amuge Rayamma, whose compositions are exclusively satirical. This story begins with the first appearance of divine love. But the path of love never runs smooth. After trials and tribulations, the bride meets the bridegroom. The start of the journey, the road and the destination: these three acts of the spiritual drama correspond to Tyaganga, Bhoganga and Yoganga suggested by the Shatsthala scheme, shorn of theological complications. The same pattern is discernible in some of the great treasures of mystical literature like Bunyan's *The Pilgrim's Progress* or Fariduddin Attar's *The Parliament of Birds*. The same pattern exists in a subtler manner in modern classics with mystical undertones like T.S. Eliot's *Four Quartets*, August Strindberg's *Road to Damascus* or Octavio Paz's *The Fable of Two Gardens*.

In the beginning, the (wo)man is kept away from the beloved by the obscuring of maya. The following vachana of Devara Dasimaiah pertains to this initial phase of the journey:

> The baby in the mother's womb
> Cannot recognize her
> Neither does the mother
> Recognize the baby.
> Deluded by maya,
> The devotees cannot see god
> Neither does god see them,
> O Ramanatha.

The following vachana by Akkamahadevi is another instance of this initial phase:

Introduction

> The deer on earth and the hare in the moon—
> What good is their love
> If they cannot mate?
> If your eyes lust in vain
> It is like a mango tree
> Bearing fruits
> Standing in a flood.
> O master Channamallikarjuna,
> I came into a world I should not have come into
> For I fell in love with the one too far away.

The struggles on the road are most movingly depicted in many of the vachanas of Akkamahadevi and in some of the vachanas of Basavanna, Revanasiddha, Allama and others. For instance:

> You parrots, chirping on by rote!
> Have you seen him? Have you?
> You, koels, singing aloud!
> Have you seen him? Have you?
> You bees, swooping, sporting!
> Have you seen him? Have you?
> You swans sporting on the lake's edge!
> Have you seen him? Have you?
> You hunting men and women
> Sporting among hills and vales.
> Have you seen him? Have you?
> Where is he,
> Channamallikarjuna, my god?
> Tell me, won't you,
> If you have seen …

Another of Akkamahadevi's vachanas, which portrays the situation, says:

> You Hunger, stand still, stand still
> You Thirst, stand still, stand still
> You Delusion, stand still, stand still
> You Lust, stand still, stand still,
> You Intoxication, stand still, stand still
> You Pride, you Hate,
> Stand still, stand still
> All of you, still and moving,
> Stand still, stand still
> I am carrying an urgent letter
> To my master, Channamallikarjuna.

Goodbye!

Consider this vachana by Revanasiddha:

> Ten types of melody have been heard
> In ten directions, have they not?
> Flowers have bloomed
> Auspiciously, have they not?
> Great joy has come
> To all peoples, has it not?
> Has he not come yet—
> The destroyer of three cities
> The master of the moon?

The arrival at the destination is dramatized in the following vachana of Goggavve's:

> Like fragrance blending with breeze
> Like pleasure blending with lovemaking
> Like the quality of giving in admiration—
> This, I say, is the path for devotees.

It is also depicted in some of the vachanas of Akkamahadevi and Devara Dasimaiah, the following vachana being an instance:

> Five elements joined together.
> The sun and the moon—are these not your bodies
> O Bull-rider?
> You have filled the world.
> If I pause to think
> Whom can I blame
> O Ramanatha?

At times, the whole journey is summed up in the same vachana, for which examples can be found in Allama and Akkamahadevi:

> Who knows of its being:
> The body of the body
> The life of life,
> The meaning of meaning?
> Thinking it far, near,
> Thinking Gogeshwara
> The Ultimate Goal
> Inside, outside,
> And unaware,
> They were robbed of everything.

Other types of vachanas can be seen as various experiences of the pilgrim en route. This is, of course, only one of the possible narratives that are in keeping with the preoccupations of the vachanakaras themselves. Other types of patterning are possible, depending on one's viewpoint.

To sum up, the theological system read into the vachanas paved the way for the creative anthologization of *Shoonya Sampadane* from which each reader can pick up hints to work out his or her own anthology of vachanas.

The extent to which a genuine Sharana needs or needs not adhere to the rules expressed in Astavarana and Panchachara provided an important subject for the vachanakaras. What is often regarded as mandatory in theology does not have a similar force in the context of the vachanas themselves that embody the experience of the vachanakaras in a deeper sense. The cracks in actual experience, which theology tries to cover up, the vachanas open up. Honest criticism of their own system is an exercise that even Basavanna, the very picture of faith, has to resort to. He observes in one of his vachanas:

> I bow down to the symbol
> When I see it.
> But, if there is no conduct
> To match the symbol,
> I sniff at it.

This is an attack on adhering to the symbol without inner worth. Similarly, the following vachana by Allama can be viewed as a critique of the mechanical worship of Istalinga without total involvement.

Introduction

> Darkness, the grasping hand, O Friend
> Darkness, the seeing eye, O Friend
> Darkness, the remembering heart, O Friend.
> All darkness, two-headed, on this side, O Friend.
> Gogeshwara's form,
> His face turned away
> Is on the other side, O Friend.

This vachana by Basavanna can be viewed as a critique of all rational theologies, including the complicated Shatsthala system:

> Can there be faith
> Without loving kindness, O Brother?
> There must be loving kindness
> For every living creature, O Brother.
>
> Loving kindness
> Is the root of all faith, O Brother
> O Kudalasangamadeva.

Though most of the vachanakaras regarded the articles of theological faith as a blueprint of their experience as (wo)men and seekers, first-hand 'seeing' was more important to their poetry than theological formulations. Nevertheless, their freedom can be clearly and concretely seen only against the background of their theology, which is one of the many contexts of their texts. The vachanas, like those of Chennabasavanna and Urilingapeddi, the two great theological poets, are over-determined by their context and, therefore, of little interest to a secular reader. On the other hand, positive and responsible critiques of the system, like most of Allama's vachanas, speak to us across centuries in an appealing tone. Familiarity with the theology of the vachanas is not essential for general readers of poetry. However, it is of great consequence to a serious student of poetry interested in the complex relationship between the two. He can gain from it insights into the ambivalent and antagonistic dependence of poetry on intellectual systems. It may also be pointed out that post-twelfth century vachanas could hardly ever match the strength of the period of its great flowering. The late vachanakaras, instead of entering into a creative dialogue with theology and ethics, take them as a priori truths, which is their last task to illuminate and demonstrate. Later vachanas have neither the sensory immediacy, nor emotional depth, nor even the intellectual courage of the twelfth-century expression.

The Context of Labour

> Kayakave Kailasa (Work itself is worship)
> —Maraiah, the rice gleaner

If the theological formulations of the Sharana movement stand for the culture of the head, its devotional and mystical poetry represents the culture of the heart. The culture of the hand is represented by the philosophy of Kayaka, literally meaning manual labour. The dictum, 'Kayakave Kailasa', a sentence taken from one of the vachanas of Maraiah, is quoted all too often in discussions and accounts of the Sharana movement and vachana philosophy. The active participation of the artisan class in the Sharana movement has already been noted. The social background of the vachanakaras is characterized by a very great diversity. It involved active participants like Basavanna, Akkamahadevi, Sakalesha Madarasa and Bonthadevi, who came from privileged castes and classes. But the whole movement was probably inaugurated not by top-ranking people but by those from the lower strata of society. The earliest poets—Chennaiah the cobbler, Dasimaiah the weaver and Ketaiah the basket maker—came clearly from artisan backgrounds. These are the predecessors mentioned with reverence time and again by Basavanna. During the heyday of the Sharana movement, both men and women of the labouring classes made significant contributions to the movement by writing vachanas and developing Basavanna's Mahamane. This was an astounding phenomenon of the period. For the men and women of this class were denied even the primary advantage of literacy in the twelfth-century caste-based social order. The activation of these classes and castes, apart from making them literate, created an atmosphere in which their creativity could flourish. Not even the twentieth century, a period when modern education has been made available to the underprivileged castes, can boast of such excellent poets and thinkers from the underprivileged castes. The social catholicity of the vachana movement is testified by the fact that individuals pursuing professions like prostitution, burglary and toddy-tapping could have access to the community of Sharanas. There were also among them a handful of Sharanas who followed the usually despised trade of street performers and buffoons. The following passage gives a fairly clear picture of the class and caste composition of the Sharana movement:

> Actually, we find many occupations mentioned in the Virashaiva literature of the twelfth century from the

highest positions in society to the lowest occupations of untouchables. There are vachanas written by a scholar (Sivalenka Mancanna), by a ruler (Sakalesa Madarasa), by a physician (Vaidya Sanganna), by a collector of taxes (Sunkada Bankanna), by a steward (Bokkasada Sanganna), by a carpenter (Baci Kayakada Basavanna), by a watchman (Talavara Kamideva), by a farmer (Okkalu Maddayya), by an umbrella holder (Sattige Kayakada Maritande), by a ferryman (Ambigara Caudayya), by a barber (Hadapada Appanna) and by a washerman (Madivala Macayya), to mention only a few of them. Among the women devotees we find spinners (Kadira Kayakada Kalavve, Kadire Remmavve), a seller of pancakes (Pittavve), rice pounders (Kottanada Remmavve, Kottanada Somamma), a rice gleaner (Aydakki Lakkamma), a sweeper (Satyakka), and a prostitute (Sule Sankavve). It remains questionable whether the wives of the high-placed men were also engaged in some form of Kayaka. However, it is clear that the Virashaiva community at Kalyana comprised a great variety of occupational activities, both of men and women. In the early hagiographic literature, we find vivid descriptions of the wide range of trades and services. For instance, the *Basavapurana* relates how Basava offers the skills of all the devotees to the Lord of the Meeting Rivers; because all work is done in His service. It results in the picture of a royal household: including a waterman, priest, garland maker, wreath maker, various ritual ministrants, firewood gatherer, forager, cook, kitchen maid, table servants, water carrier, quid supplier, food taster, physician, puppeteer, singer, jester, reader, poet, scholar, musicians, accountant, commander-in-chief, minister, chief of the elephant corps, equerry, attendant, pimp,

Introduction

companion, bodyguard, standard bearer, servant, tax collector, dagger carrier, story teller, nurse, exorcist, timekeeper, lancer, mistress, bond servant, merchant, washerman, lamp carrier, white washer, potter, hunter, blacksmith, herdsman, palanquin bearer, storekeeper, milkman, and milk boiler. Thus all vocations are performed by the devotees with a distinct goal: the service of the Lord.[16]

It may also be added that more than fifty per cent of vachanakaras came from the artisan classes. The participation of labouring and toiling people in such a large number is related to the significance attached to material life in vachana lore. Most of the devotional and mystical schools of thought in India preach an otherworldly philosophy that regards material pursuits as anti-spiritual. By contrast, the Sharanas preached an inclusive type of spirituality that considers the human body as a temple and the world of humans as 'the mint of the Maker'. Though the ritualistic and overly theological viewpoints represented by Chennabasavanna and Urilingapeddi, the esoteric and mystical views found in Allama and Madhuvaiah, the god-intoxicated devotion of Akkamahadevi and Gajesha Masanaiah are expressions of perspectives of equal significance in the Sharana movement, its artisan class context seems its most unique feature. The episodes concerning Maraiah, the rice gleaner, and Chandaiah, the rope maker in *Shoonya Sampadane* suggest that debates frequently occurred in Anubhava Mantapa, the Hall of Experience, about the

---

[16]Johan Peter Schouten, *Revolution of Mystics*, 1991, Kok Pharos Publishing House, Kampen, pp. 27–28.

comparative merits of the labour-as-worship proper. Dhoolaiah, the cobbler, goes to the extent of treating labour as superior to devotion. Even Basavanna, though not a member of the labouring class, attached a very high significance to labour.

Another outcome of the same factor is seen in the fact that attacks against discrimination provided one of the most recurrent themes for the vachanakaras. Whatever their class background, the vachanakaras are united in their rejection of caste hierarchy. Brahmins, the chief beneficiaries of the caste system, are often the butt of attack. Even otherworldly poets like Allama express their disapproval of caste discrimination. Both men and women of all castes were welcome to join the Sharana community, a fact testified by the overwhelming presence of the lower castes and classes among the vachanakaras. However, this attitude was not without its negative consequences. It led to a vertical division of (wo)man-kind into Bhaktas and Bhavis, as mutually exclusive species. Bhaktas included all Sharanas, irrespective of caste. Bhavis consisted of not only all atheists and worldlings but members of other faiths, no matter how pious. Basavanna refers to the emperor, Bijjala, as a Bhavi in spite of the fact that Bijjala was an ardent devotee of Shiva for the simple reason that he was not a follower of the Sharana path. What a contrast to his emphasis on loving-kindness for all creatures in his vachanas! The most militant spokesman of the community like Machaiah the washerman, and Chowdaiah the ferryman, are full of admonitions against having any truck with the customs, rites and gods of Bhavis.

The crisis of transition from their original ethos to the new ethos are expressed in the vachanas by Bommaiah the drummer, Bummatadeva, a former Jaina and Manchanna, a former Vaishnava. Bommaiah's admittance into the Sharana fold did not stop him from continuing to make his living out of worshipping the village goddess Mari, who is often the object of the Sharanas' contempt.

Another interesting implication of the context of labour is the inflow of new metaphors into vachana poetry. The vachanakaras in general and those from the labouring classes in particular are rich in metaphors of this kind. Apart from giving the idiom of the vachanas concreteness and experiential authenticity, such metaphors help them integrate the seen and the unseen worlds in their compositions. This phenomenon is illustrated by the vachana of Chennaiah, the cobbler, already quoted. This also comes alive in the following vachana of Dhoolaiah, the cobbler:

> On seeing the great godhead
> Appear on the edge of the chisel
> Piercing the hide—
> 'Why are you here, sir
> In front of the one that moves about
> Carrying the bag of flesh?
> Go go away
> To the dwelling places of your devotees
> Free them
> Go on to the top of your silver mountain,
> With your masquerades
> Go free your devotees.
> By the grace of the master of lust, dust and smoke
> Go and prosper.'

Most of the spiritual paths in India divided a (wo)man into two irreconciliable halves: the spiritual and the material. A good deal of vachana poetry also represents the conflicting claims of the spirit and the flesh as in the vachana of Basavanna, which likens the body to a temple and to Kailasa, the state of liberation, also called bodily existence, a snake basket. Such vacillations and conflicts are rare in poets from the labouring classes. Wedded to the practice of labour as a mode of soteriology, they celebrate worldly existence through their metaphors taken from their walks of life. In their poetry, spiritual endeavour and physical labour are co-terminous. They have a work ethic-based salvific approach to spirituality markedly different from those of Basavanna, Akkamahadevi or Allama. It is the artisan Sharanas who are mordantly critical of lethargic and false Jangamas trying to fleece them. Even Allama, the unquestioned leader of the Sharanas, was challenged by the much lesser figure of a rope maker. He asks the mendicant Allama what his profession was when Allama was trying to convince him that the worship of Linga is as important as labour.

On the face of it, Kayaka philosophy appears to be similar to Karmayoga, preached in the Bhagavad Gita. However, Karmayoga was part of the Varnashrama social order. The philosophy of Kayaka was part of an ethos opposed to the caste system. Further, it is closely related to the ethical component of Sharana theology as represented in Sadachara. The theoretical insistence that Sharanas are entitled to the proceeds of their labour is clear from the episode of Maraiah the rice gleaner, in *Shoonya Sampadane*. The Sharanas rejected charity for they, as a group, declared themselves against the classes and institutions that had fattened themselves on charity—Brahmins and temple priests. Frequent injunctions in the vachanas against 'parasati, paradhana, paradaiva' (another's wife, another's money, another's god) is also noteworthy here. The social idealism of well-meaning artisan Sharanas notwithstanding, there is evidence in vachana literature that hangers-on and spongers were mushrooming even in the community of Sharanas. In later Virashaiva works, including the post-twelfth-century vachanas, the highly original Kayaka philosophy was gradually marginalized as the active participation of lower castes in shaping Virashaiva philosophy almost ceased after the twelfth century.

The Context of Performance

Vachanas are not poems composed primarily as reading texts. The language of the vachanas is inscribed with grammatical markers such as vocatives, imperatives and interjections, which indicate that they were composed in the dialogic setting of Anubhava Mantapa rather than in the individual isolation of the poets. One of the vachanakaras of the period, Shantarasa, the librarian of the vachanas, was assigned the task of recording and compiling vachanas spontaneously composed by poets during their interaction with each other and with others both in Anubhava Mantapa and in the course of their daily lives. Further, the composition and recitation of the vachanas appear to have been a performance. The free verse pattern of the vachanas makes them flexible, lending themselves to a variety of verbal and non-verbal performances. To this day, both Hindustani and Carnatic singers use vachana texts as compositions for their recitals.[17] A few dance recitals have also been based on them in recent times.[18]

We have reasons to assume that the vachanas were both sung out and performed during the twelfth century. Allama mentions in a vachana of his that he was in the habit of composing vachanas while singing. Most of the vachanakaras, apart from composing vachanas in free verse, have composed the vachana-like songs called Swaravachanas. vachanas were neutral with respect to performance whereas Swaravachanas were exclusively composed for song performances.[19]

There was also a handful of poets who were performers of different kinds. Chowdaiah of many guises, Maritande, the clown, and Kalaketaiah were street performers by profession. These poets, the first two in particular, draw upon their professional details in the vachanas. Chowdaiah's vachanas indicate that he composed vachanas while acting out his street performances. He makes frequent references to donning and doffing various guises including those of well-known Sharanas. Maritande, true to his clownish performances, employs numerous details to convey spiritual experiences.

Two other performer-poets of the period are Bommaiah the drummer, and Bommaiah the Kinnari player. Bommaiah the drummer appears to have been a holy beggar, who carried

---

[17] Mallikarjun Mansoor, the famous Hindustani vocalist, has popularized the vachanas through his art round the country. B. Devendrappa set vachanas to the ragas of Carnatic classical music. Honnappa Bhagavathar was also an expert in singing vachanas in the Carnatic style.

[18] Such dance recitals have been performed mainly by classical dancers like Sharada Rudra, Vyjayanti Kashi and Suma Vasanth.

[19] L. Basavaraju, introduction to *Shivadasa Gitanjali*, op. cit.

on his head the image of Mari, one of the lower deities often mocked at by the vachanakaras in their monotheistic fervour. He went around begging, playing the dakke. Bommaiah, the Kinnari player, on the other hand, earned his living by playing on his string instrument in front of a temple. vachanas by both poets show the influence of their respective professions.[20]

Before winding up the discussion of contexts, it should be pointed out that Bommaiah the drummer shows the ambivalence characteristic of the transition from one culture to another. He tries in his vachana to imbue with Sharana mystical significance the culture of Mari worship, which is condemned as gross superstition by vachanakaras in general. Similarly, ambivalences are seen in the vachanas of Manumuni Gummatadeva, a convert from Jainism and those of Gupta Manchanna, a convert from Vaishnavism. Like Bommaiah, the drummer, they also try to reconcile their old culture with the new. The vachanas of such poets show that bi-culturalism is another intriguing context of the vachana movement.

The Context of Vachana Translations

As a species of translated literature, the vachanas, in turn, lend themselves to further translations. A strong element of intertextuality in twelfth-century vachanas suggests that the vachanakaras often translated compositions of each other. Consider the following vachana of Akkamahadevi, a stock theme in vachanas:

[20] For a detailed discussion on this subject, refer to H.S. Shivaprakash, *Sahitya Mattu Rangabhoomi*, 1993, Karnataka Sahitya Academy, Bangalore, pp. 79–86 and 101–103.

> Like treasure hiding in the earth
> Like taste hiding in the fruit
> Like gold hiding in the stone
> Like oil hiding in sesame
> Like fire hiding in the tree
> No one can see Channamallikarjuna—
> The Brahmin hiding in yearning.

This has several versions in other poets like Allama and Basavanna. Among swaravachanas, one finds quite a few translations of prose vachanas. In post-fifteenth-century hagiographic literature on the Sharanas, like Chamarasa's *Prabhulingaleele*, there are several translations of the vachanas into stanzaic forms. Intralingual translation of the vachanas can be found in some of the compositions of the Haridasas of the sixteenth century.

After their brief but magnificent efflorescence in the twelfth century, the vachanas went underground for over a couple of centuries to be retrieved, compiled, commented upon and anthologized in the fifteenth century during the reign of Praudadevaraya, the Vijayanagara emperor. This process continued in the sixteenth century under the saintly inspiration of Tontadarya.

Though printing technology was initiated in Karnataka around 1817, as part of Christian missionary zeal, ancient Kannada works began to be published in 1837. European and British scholars took a deep interest in Kannada by way of producing dictionaries, grammars, editing folk texts, including hagiographic Virashaiva texts like *Chennabasavapurana* and *Basavapurana*. Kittel, the first lexicographer in Kannada, was acquainted with the vachanakaras. On the whole, Christian missionaries evinced no interest in publishing vachanas.[21] The publication of vachana texts began gradually in the second half of the last century. However, Pha Gu Halakatti was the first dedicated scholar who spent a whole lifetime's energy searching, recovering, compiling and editing vachanas. He first approached the Basel Mission Press, Mangalore, for the publication of vachana texts, which he offered to finance as well. Months later they wrote back: 'Because, in this work of yours the same teachings have been propounded which are also propounded in our faith, its publication may come in the way of the propagation of our faith.'[22] In short, Christian missionaries ignored the vachana texts out of missionary zeal.

In the meantime, the Virashaiva community was strengthening its economic and socio-political power. Various Virashaiva organizations and individuals were fired with missionary enthusiasm. Virashaiva scholars like Halakatti and S.S. Basavanal laboured hard to edit texts from palm-leaf manuscripts scattered all over Karnataka. Later, publication wings of Karnataka University, Dharwar, took up vachana publication in a big way during the 1950s and the 60s.

This process synchronized with many non-Virashaiva scholars, particularly Brahmins, taking interest in vachana lore for two reasons; namely, to understand vachanas as an extension of Hinduism, and to underline the literary value of vachanas. Chief among these scholars were Srinivasamurthy, R.R. Diwakar and A.N. Krishna Rao. After the 1960s, there has been a rise in non-Virashaiva scholarship on the vachanas. Literacy among

[21]B.V. Mallapur, 'Prarambhada Prayatnagala Prathama Ghatta,' in M.M. Kalburgi (ed.), *Vachana Sahityada Prakataneya Itihasa*, 1991, Veerashaiva Adhyayana Samsthe, Gadag, pp. 2–3.
[22]Ibid.

the backwards and dalits has led to analyses of the vachanas from these viewpoints. Such works underline the socio-political aspects of the vachanas more than the literary. In recent decades, European scholars like Shouten and Blake Michael have also done scholarly studies of Virashaivism. Their interests are basically from the vantage points of human sciences.

Following the publication of A.K. Ramanujan's English translations of the vachanas in 1973, Anglophone scholars have been evincing interest in the vachanas. This period coincides with the shift in emphasis from Sanskrit as the paradigm of Indian literature to vernacular literatures of India.

On the whole, the emphasis on vachana scholarship has centred on Virashaiva missionary zeal, the representation of the vachanas as a version of reformatory Hinduism, the literariness of the vachanas, and their radical potential and socio-political aspects of vachanas. Virashaiva missionary zeal is characteristic of works produced by the nexus of Virashaiva scholars and institutions of the community while the focus on reformatory Hinduism and the literariness of the vachanas has been the forte of Brahmins. The literariness of the vachanas has also been the focus of attention of secular Virashaiva scholars, and scholars of backward and dalit communities and their works betray their preoccupation with the radical potentials of the vachanas. European scholars have largely focused on the socio-political aspects of vachanas. The above tendencies are often found together in the same scholars.

These types of vachana scholarship have implications for the different translations of the vachanas. The early translations by K.R. Srinivasa Iyengar and Basavannal represent a mixture of the first and second trends. A.K. Ramanujan's translations represent the third and fifth trends. My interest has been a combination of the third, fourth and fifth trends.

Ramanujan wrongly suggested that the vachanakaras used 'substandard dialects'. On the contrary, what vachanakaras did was to inscribe substandard speech modes into the standard Kannada of their times. He has suggested elsewhere that they spoke in the mother tongue, Kannada instead of in the father tongue, Sanskrit.[23] However, they enriched the father-Kannada with various mother-Kannadas. While translating them here, an attempt is made to emulate their practice of dislocating our father tongue, the English language. The English and English poetry have rewritten us long enough. Let us now rewrite them on our terms. In the process, we are also recreating ourselves.

---

[23] A.K. Ramanujan, 'Talking to God in the Mother Tongue', *Manushi*. 5 April 2007, online at <http://www.manushi-india.org/pdfs_issues/articles/Talking%20to%20God%20in%20Mother%20Tongue.pdf>.

Abbreviations of the Kannada Source Texts

Akkana Vachanagalu—AV
Akkagala Vachanagalu—AGV
Allama Prabhu Devara Vachanagalu—APV
Allamana Vachana Chandrike—AVC
Basavannavara Shatsthalada Vachanagalu—BSV
Basavannanavara Shatsthalada Vachanagalu—BSV-LB
Bedagina Vachanagalu—BV
Devara Dasimaiah Vachanagalu—DDV
Mahadeviyakkana Vachanagalu—MV
Sakala Purathanara Vachanagalu—SPV
Sakala Purathanara Vachanagalu-2—SPV-2
Sakala Purathanara Vachanagalu-3—SPV-3
Samagra Vachana Samputa—SVS-1–15
Sri Siddharameshwara Vachanagalu—SSV
Vachana Kammata—VK
Veerashaiva Sulnudikaararu—VS

The Path: Vachanas

Adaiah:

Four Vedas are similes:
So are sixteen Shastras
Eighteen Puranas
Twenty-eight sacred Agamas
Thirty-two Upanishads
Seven million great mantras.
Similes, all just similes
Countless words, scriptures,
Systems of logic and grammar—
Similes
Many many mantras, tantras
The mastery of yantras or black magic—
Similes.
Hearing the unheard
Attaining the unattainable
Penetrating the impenetrable—
Similes, always.
Unable to stop similes
Unable to transcend the web of similes
Unable to free themselves
From the thick paste of similes and non-similes
Unable to prevent the contamination of feelings
Thought forming or not,
Unable to see the truth

Of Sowrashtra Someshwara
These simile-bound people
Make similes with similes
Come into being through similes.

(SVS-4 31)

Siddharama:

The vachana experience
Is not a construct of speech, O my heart.
It is not a construct of speech
*Vachananubhavo vacho naiva**
This is established in the revelations
O Kapilasiddhamallikarjuna.

(SSV 307)

---

* The Vachana experience is not to be spoken about.

Machideva, the washerman:

The vain entertainers
Who speak strings of vachanas
Are they devotees, O Friend?
Vachanas are not like them
Neither are they like vachanas.
The reason is this—
At their back
Only the concerns of flesh and fortune
In front of them
Just a haystack of words.
Like a dog wagging its tail
When he sees his master,
Their words.
O father Kalidevaradeva.

(SPV-3 210)

The Path:
I Saw This Wonder

Akkamahadevi:

As you are like water in milk
I do not know
What's first, what's next
What is master, what is slave,
O Channamallikarjuna
By singing your praises with love
Will not an ant become Rudra?

(AV 35)

Akkamahadevi:

Five kinds of garments given to me
Turn into the cow with four udders
A calf was born of the cow's womb
And the cow was milked
Without letting the calf touch it,

The milk tasted so sweet.

Sweetness gone to the head, and
All usefulness cast off,
When I followed the cow,
Birth and death ended,
Channamallikarjuna.

(MV 100)

Allama Prabhu:

When clouds brought downpour
In the north country
Famine struck the land
And all the beasts died.

On the ground of their cremation
I will look for you, Gogeshwara.

(APV 93)

Allama Prabhu:

If the hill feels cold,
With what will they cover it, O Friend?
If space stays naked,
With what will they clothe it, O Friend?
If the worshipper turns worldly
To what shall I compare him, O Gogeshwara?

(AVC 26)

Allama Prabhu:

Eating from the skull, playing in graveyards:
That's his anti-normal nature.
Hard, hard to penetrate, this expert
Gogeshwara alone is an outcaste
Polluted, all the rest.

(AVC 178)

Allama Prabhu:

Pictures drawn on three canvases—
The first stays
The second keeps going and coming
The third goes away
And does not return.
O Gogeshwara,
Your Sharana is beyond these three types.

(AVC 92)

Allama Prabhu:

Coming without invitation
Leaving without leave
No one notices
Not even birds and beasts that arrive every day
All those who came
Left after bathing and eating. But
Gogeshwaralinga leaves without eating—
This no one notices.

(AVC 10)

Allama Prabhu:

Our men sow gardens
Java's* men give it protection
O inconstant world
The fire lit up by Gogeshwara
Is for burning,
Not for cooking.

(AVC 11)

---

*Yama, the god of death.

Allama Prabhu:

The deer with the tiger's head
The tiger with the deer's head
The two—joined at the waist—
It is not the tiger, not the deer
But something else
Come to eat next. Look!
When the body without the head
Grazes—
Look, O Gogeshwara,
The leaf vanishes.

(AVC 24)

Allama Prabhu:

I saw, O Friend
A monkey fondling an elephant
That had dropped dead.
I saw, O Friend
A harlot in a forest calling men
And pawning herself.
I saw, O Friend
Dogs quarrelling in a ravaged town.
What is this wonder, O Gogeshwara?

(AVC 12)

I Saw This Wonder

Allama Prabhu:

Look! The sight of Rahu
Swallowing the deer in the moon
Haunts me day after day.

Look! The belly of one
Being the head of another
Haunts me day after day.

But, today, joy comes swallowing joy
Looking for the earth below.
How shall I depict
Today's constellations of suns and moons
O Gogeshwara?

(AVC 7)

Allama Prabhu:

Tell me
What were you
Before I knew myself?
Earlier, you had kept your mouth shut
This I have seen in your eyes.

If you open your mouth
Now that I have known myself
I see it with my eyes
And feel shy. Look!
The vision that holds together
You looking at me
And me looking at you
Is one
Look!
Look, O Gogeshwara.
I have realized the skill of your strange beauty.

(AVC 4)

I Saw This Wonder

Allama Prabhu:

Sunrise, is it?
Sundown, over?
Ah, they have vanished,
All formations made of water
Darkness caved
In all the three worlds
Tell me
What is the enigma
Of all this, O Gogeshwara?

(AVC 10)

Allama Prabhu:

In the quietness of contemplation
Many strange wonders:

On the curtain wide as the sky
On the sacred canopy wide as the world
Seeing the vision, truth of truths,
I saw
The sunrise
In the majesty of the sky,
Having become
Gogeshwara himself.

(AVC 97)

Allama Prabhu:

On the field without earth
The man without eyes found diamonds.
Another without hands strung them together
Another without a neck wore it,
O Gogeshwara,
Is there ever ruin
To beauty lacking the body?

(AVC 97)

Allama Prabhu:

When acting
One must act the act violating the act, dear one.
When speaking
One must speak the speech violating the speech, dear one.
When holding the body
One must hold it without holding it, dear one.
When mating
One must mate the mating without violating, dear one.
O Gogeshwara
When standing still
One must stand still in
You.

(APV 482)

Allama Prabhu:

The earth and the sky are
Stomached in a living thing.
Tell me,
What is great here
To him that does not call it great?
Tell me,
What is trivial here
To him that does not call it trivial?
If greatness enters the heart
Is there anything like it
O Gogeshwara?

(APV 12)

Allama Prabhu:

In the infinite dark,
Who placed the inordinate light,
Its opposite?
Darkness is
Light
Is
Itself—
The same!
There!
What kind of marvel is this?
One is not afraid of the other.

Seeing
The elephant and the lion
Together
Feeding
I was amazed,
O Gogeshwara.

(APV 183)

Allama Prabhu:

While stepping back
To watch your splendour
It was
Like a hundred billion suns rising, O Father.
It was
Like cutting through the maze
Of lightning creepers,
Lifting up the root,
Looking at it, O Father
O Gogeshwara.
If you become a linga of flame
No one can compare and see, O Father.

(APV 1179)

Allama Prabhu:

In the eyes' forest
In the midst of the town
Five corpses are lying
They keep coming
Weeping
The kinsmen
Because they are
So many
So great
The firewood will not be put out
Neither will the corpse burn up
Only the bier is in flames
O Gogeshwara.

(AVC 26)

Basavanna:

You can make people speak,
People bitten by snakes or possessed,
But not people possessed by riches, O Brother.

When poverty—the magician—walks in,
They too will begin to speak,
O Kudalasangama.

(BSV 35)

Basavanna:

On the Jambu island
Among nine continents:
'I'll kill you'—the voice of god;
'I'll survive'—the voice of his devotee.
Your good devotees win the day
With the sharp blade of truth
Look! Kudalasangama.

(BSV 179)

Basavanna:

Wide as the world, wide as the sky,
Wider still, your wideness
Further, further below the underworld
Your sacred feet
Further, further, above the cosmic egg
Your sacred crown
O master Kudalasanga, O Linga
Unknown, unfelt, unequalled,
Resting on my palm, you have become so tiny.

(BSV 48)

Basavanna:

Look!
Living beyond the slightest trace
Of all darkness!
Light, becoming a throne to light!
Only Kudalasangama the father sees ...

(BSV 264)

Revanasiddha:

Tell me, O master Revana
What is this wonder—
Conquering time, karma, birth
The sight rapt in surrounding space,
The hearing lost in space above,
The whimpering absorbed in contentment
In mind-stuff, beyond body?

(vs 40)

Dasimaiah, the weaver:

You put inside the tree hollow
Slow fire that does not burn
You put into milk
The ghee that does not show
You put into the body
The soul that is not seen
I marvel at the ways
Of your composition, O Ramanatha.

(DDV 57)

Dasimaiah, the weaver:

Five elements joined together.
The sun and the moon—
Are these not your bodies
O Bull-rider?
You have filled the world.
If I pause to think
Whom can I blame
O Ramanatha?

(DDV 67)

Maritande, the clown:

When,
After having seen all sorts of people,
I went to her,
Before I sat down
She kicked me
Teeth fell out of my mouth,
My chin was broken
My tongue shrank,
O Mareshwara, foe of haste.

(VK 439)

Maritande, the clown:

The lord of Delhi died
At the hands of a village pariah
The weeping husband became
The wife's meanest slave
The master changed into a bull
So that the slave could ride on him;
A sheaf of hay mowed down the sword's hilt,
O Mareshwara, foe of haste.

(SPV 314)

Gangambike:

Ah!
A tiger came
From a desolate land
To eat my young calf
The tiger couldn't return
To the desolate land
The tiger looked at the young calf
And turned into a mother.
What shall I say of this?
O Kudalsangamadeva, dear to Ganga!

(SVS-5 218)

The Path: Ugh! This Empty Show of the World

Akkamahadevi:

Ugh! This empty show of the world
First he comes, the masked one.
Saying, 'O Father, Papa.'
Next comes a moustache-masked one,
Daubed with ghee.
At the end comes a mask of old, old age
The moment your eyesight ceases
The dance of the world stops
O Channamallikarjuna.

(MV 10)

Akkamahadevi:

Hills have no sap in them, they say
Tell me, sir, how else are trees born there?
Charcoal has no liquid in it, they say
Tell me, sir, how else does iron melt in it?
I have no body, they say.
Tell me, sir, how else does Channamallikarjuna live in me?

(SVS-5 78)

Akkamahadevi:

O Father,
Is it proper to poison the baby
Fed on the drink of immortals?
O Father,
Is it proper
To put a fence of flames
Around a plant grown in the cooling shade?
Is it proper, O Channamallikarjuna,
To let a murderous butcher
Talk to the baby of your compassion?

(AV 14)

Akkamahadevi:

To a man
Self-hood appearing as a woman's affection,
Begins to haunt him. Look!
Maya haunts the heart as memory,
Memory as awareness
And herds of the whole world
As a shepherd's whiplash.

O Channamallikarjuna,
No one can conquer
The maya you have unfurled.

(AV 33)

Akkamahadevi:

Look, all of you
All the Vedas, Shastras, Agamas, Puranas
Are the grit and husk
From beaten paddy.
Why beat it? Why strike it?
Once you purge the mind
From flowing here and there,
Pure light dawns,
Channamallikarjuna.

(MV 102)

I Keep Vigil of Rudra

Akkamahadevi:

A fisherman, after entering the water
And searching, rejoices at killing
Many creatures.
Why does he not grieve for them
As he would if his baby died
In his own house?
Put another way:
*Swa'manamitaram cheti bhinnata naiva drishyatam
Surva chijyotireveti yah pasyati sa pasyati.**
Laughing stock in the eyes of the world—
The grief of the fisherman.
For this reason,
What shall I call those madigas
Who, though devotees of Channamallikarjuna,
Are cruel to other lives?

(MV 49)

---

*He who realizes all as divine life sees no distinction between the self and the other.

Akkamahadevi:

If you can pull out the serpent's fangs
And make it dance
It is good to make friends with serpents.
If you can describe the body's composition
It is good to make friends with the body.
Like a mother turned into a she-monster
Body's sickness.
O Channamallikarjuna,
Don't say those you love
Have a body.

(MV 39)

Allama Prabhu:

When the camphor hill catches fire
Does the charcoal remain?
Does the snow-built Shiva temple
Have a sunlight cupola?

When a hill of cinders is shot
With a wax arrow
Why look for the arrow again?
After seeing Gogeshwara
Why remember him again?

(APV 242)

Allama Prabhu:

Why be a captive of the bed
While mating in love?
Does one in rut
Ever feel shy?
Why the worry and craving for worship
For the Sharana that knows you?
Why the need of touchstone
For pure, shining gold?
Is there even a sign
For Gogeshwaralinga?

(VK 18)

Allama Prabhu:

Listen, all of you
You who claim to not touch flesh and wine.
Are not the eight types of intoxication wine?
Are not worldly ties flesh?
Only he that cuts off both
Becomes one with Linga,
Is Gogeshwaralinga.

(VK 26)

Allama Prabhu:

You can offer the word
Not the word's substance.
You can make a rice offering
Not the offering of the offered.
Gogeshwara,
Your Sharanas look back,
Make an offering of the 'ahead'.

(AVC 40)

Allama Prabhu:

Objective poetry, subjective poetry,
Naturalistic poetry—
Words spoken on these three foundations
Are on this side.

Who knows them on the other side,
Beyond?

The people do not even know where it is,
These, prattling like a flock of parrots—
However, can such ones know you
O Gogeshwara?

(AVC 96)

Basavanna:

They do not believe, do not trust
But call out in vain
They do not know how to believe
These men of the world.
If they call out, believing,
Will not Shiva say: 'Yes?'
To men who merely call out
But do not believe
Says Kudalasangama, our father:
'Go on, blow your horn, go on crying out.'

(BSV 13)

Basavanna:

Yes, you can stand around
When the oven is burning
But where can you flee
When the whole earth is burning?
When the bank drinks up the water
And the fence grazes the field,
And the housewife steals from her own house,
And the mother's poisoned breast milk kills,
O Kudalasangamadeva
To whom shall I complain?

(BSV 8)

Basavanna:

They trapped the hill, O Brother
And stretched before me
The net of sins.
The hunter came, chasing the beast,
The beast now inside the tomb.
The beast caught in the net of Hara
Became a dish
For our Kudalasangamadeva.

(BSV 14)

Basavanna:

Like the dog on the palanquin,
This heart
Does not give up the old ways.
The moment it sees you know what
It goes back to its old ways.
O burn, burn this heart.
That runs towards sensual things
But does not let me remember.

Day after day, you, O Master
O my master Kudalasangama
Be so kind that I may remember
Your feet—I beg, I pray.

(BSV 189)

Basavanna:

What if you go riding the elephant?
What if you go riding the horse?
What if you go wearing
Vermilion and Kasturi scent
O Brother?
O you have gone without realizing
The essence of truth
O you have gone without sowing or reaping
The yield of virtue
O riding the inebriated elephant of pride
You have become destiny's target
O without seeing our lord
Kudalasangama
You have become a target for hell.

(BSV 168)

Basavanna:

Look at this—
The snake charmer and his broken-nosed wife,
Snake in their hands,
Go to check omens for their son's wedding.
They exclaim, 'Bad omen! Let's not . . .'
On the road another snake charmer
And his broken-nosed wife!
Broken-nosed, one's own wife!
Snakes, in one's own hands, too!
Himself, broken nosed!
What shall I call such a cur
Blind to one's own faults
Yet calling others names,
O Kudalasangamadeva?

(BSV 28)

Basavanna:

Earth is one and the same
For pariah street
And Shiva temple;
Water is one and the same
For washing shit
And ritual cleaning;
All castes are one
For a man with self-knowledge
Salvation's fruit is one and the same
For all six systems;
Truth is one,
O master Kudalasangama
For the one who knows you.

(BSV 241)

Basavanna:

All other men have gone hunting
Why haven't you, O my husband?
Do not bring any dead thing
Do not kill with your hands
Do not return without meat.
If, in god's bounty,
The prey comes your way,
Let us offer it
To lord Kudalasangama
O my husband.

(BSV 249)

Basavanna:

When you look at a stone snake
'Give it a drink of milk,' they say, O Friend.
When they see a real snake
'Kill it,' they say, O Friend.
When a Jangama comes, ready to eat,
'Get out,' they say.
For the Linga that cannot eat,
'Bring rice,' they say, O Friend.
When they see the Sharanas of Kudalasangama
And show neglect
They will become like a lump of earth
Smashed by stone.

(BSV 50)

Basavanna:

Slogging slogging
They became ruined
They slogged without the heart.
Giving, giving
They became ruined
They gave without the truth.
If they have virtue and truth
While slogging and giving
Our Master Kudalasangama
Will be with them.

(BSV 60)

Basavanna:

O Man,
The affairs of kings
The show of wealth
Are not constant.
Look—
Kalyana was doomed, devastated

Because of the pride of a single Jangama
The rule of the Chalukya king was ended.

It went into your begging bowl of human skull
O master Kudalasangama.

(BSV 165)

Goggavve:

If a man grows fond of a woman
And clutches her
That thing must be seen as another's belonging.
If a woman grows fond of a man
And clutches him
How is this to be seen?
If, shedding both his and her
If the self can be content, I call it master of nothing self-complete.

(vs 318)

Siddharama:

A cock crows
Day in and day out

They do not heed it
The multitudes of dying men

If you understand
No birth, no bondage for you.
If you do not,
No end to your births and deaths

O Kapilasiddhamallikarjuna.

(VK 77)

Siddharama:

Life is like a lamp
You never know
How it comes
How it goes
Life is like a cloud
You never know
How it comes
How it goes
Life is like an infant
You never know
If it is alive
If it will go on living
Look, Kapilasiddhamallikarjuna!

(SSV 24)

Dasimaiah, the weaver:

To the gift of elephants
I will say no
To the gift of a huge fortune
I will say no
To the gift of a vast empire
I will say no
But, to the gift of the wise sayings
Of your devotees,
Just for a moment
I will even give you away
O Ramanatha.

(DDV 56)

Dasimaiah, the weaver:

When the lamp goes out,
Where does the light hide?
When the body gives way
Where does the soul hide?
I challenge those who can penetrate
This secret, O Ramanatha.

(DDV 58)

Dasimaiah, the weaver:

The baby in the mother's womb
Cannot recognize her
Neither does the mother
Recognize the baby.
Deluded by maya,
The devotees cannot see god
Neither does god see them,
O Ramanatha.

(DDV 62)

Dasimaiah, the weaver:

He filled a tattered bag with paddy
And walked all night
He was afraid to have to pay the toll
The paddy was all gone
Only the bag remained.
Such is the devotion, O Ramanatha,
Of the weak hearted.

(DDV 67)

Dasimaiah, the weaver:

The man with a body grows hungry
The man with a body tells lies
Do not tease me,
The man with a body
Just once
Take on a body like mine
And see for yourself, O Ramanatha.

(DDV 85)

Dasimaiah, the weaver:

Your gift, the earth;
Your gift, the harvest;
Your gift, the wind that blows about.
These men who enjoy your gifts
And praise others—
What shall I call these curs
O Ramanatha?

(DDV 76)

Lingamma, the virtuous wife of Hadapada Appanna:

O all humans of the mortal world are dead,
Drowned in darkness
Having learned how to speak
Uttering anxious words lost by a mouth full of holes
Fond of the well of piss and the pond of shit
Biting each other, driven mad—
The donkey-men wander.
Chennabasavanna, dear to Appanna
Does not approve of them.

(SVS-5 340)

Molige Mahadevi:

Sir, why all this chatter
About being established
In union with Shiva?
This is no play of eternal truths
This stunt you indulge in
Who has given you permission?
Who are you going to tell this to?
Tell me
Who do you think you are?
Be aware of that feeling
Know yourself,
O beloved of my lord
Mallikarjuna, of two-fold purity.

(SVS-5 283)

Molige Mahadevi:

Holding a lamp in one's hands
Why speak of darkness?
Carrying the essence of touchstone in one's hand,
Why toil like a coolie?
Once hunger disappears
Why carry the weight of delicious food?
After seeing the enduring and the unenduring
It is not proper for devotees
To speak of the mortal world and Kailasa.

See yourself by yourself—
In the beloved of my master Mallikarjuna
Of two-fold purity,
That completely naked light.

(SVS-5 291)

Machideva, the washerman:

O Shiva,
Free and beyond maya!
The light you spat out
Became spittle.
A wonder of wonders, this!
From the drop of your spittle—
Primordial sound, dot and forms were born.
From the web of your spittle,
Men and women were born
Who bore many children
Who bore five children.
People who garnished their food
With your spittle—
Their eyes were blinded.
O Kalidevardeva, I have realized this.

(SVS 278)

Chennabasavanna:

They measure the heap
Of a life
With huge jars of
The sunrise and the sunset.
Before the heap is emptied
Give up
The false shows of pleasures.
Offer
Worship to Shivalinga
Whoever does not
Goes to the worst hell.

(VK 71)

Chennabasavanna:

Can you draw water from the depths
Without rope
Without the help of steps?
Look, all of you,
The people building word-steps
To lead us—
These are the devotees of old.
To remove the dirt from the heart
Of those in the dying world
They lit the lamps
Of songs and utterances—
Devotees of Kudalachannasanga.

(VK 1)

Urilingadeva:

Men can give warmth to the body:
But tell me girl, dear friend,
Can they give warmth to the heart?
Nowhere have I seen such a beauty
Nowhere, such a man
Nowhere, such a wonder
He gave to my heart the warmth of virtue
He, Urilingadeva, so beautiful to me.

(SPV-1 414)

Urilingadeva:

Thinking that my love doesn't love me
I got angry and started to hide
Look O Mother
All my hiding places were only he!
No place is without you, O Love
What good is my anger
If there is no place to hide?
I shall surrender myself up to him.
To Urilingadeva.

(VK 388)

Kalavve, the pious wife of Urilingapeddi:

They say—
All those are high born
Who eat sheep, fowl and tiny fish,
They say—
All those are low born
Who eat the cow that rains on Shiva
Sacred milk sanctified five times.
What the Brahmins had eaten adorned the grass
And a dog licked it up and went away.
What the cobblers had eaten adorned the grass—
Now Brahmins' ornament.
In other words
Bags are made of cow's hide
For ghee and for water.
Senseless Brahmins who drink
Ghee and water from such leather bags
Thinking it sacred
They can't escape
Utmost perdition.
The master of Urilingapeddi
Doesn't approve of such men.

(SVS-5 206)

Ghattivalaiah:

A sacrificial pit in the middle of the village—
All pious ones made offerings

Look, the world has turned into smoke,
The laughing stock of the smokeworld.

When laugh and smoke
Turn into smoke
Smoke turns into the world.
I declare—
Never, never!
Siddalinga, dear to Chikkaiah.

(SPV-1 246)

Shantarasa, the treasurer of vachanas:

Like the impatience of the man
Who can't wait till what's hidden is revealed—
Watching the play of guises behind a curtain
Or the hidden part behind a sari.
My restlessness . . .
Show me
Your true form
Hidden in stone.
Rid me
Of my stone heart.
O master of my heart,
O emptiness unwritten,
O sound unheard.
Give up
The wickedness of the burning stone
I beg of you.

(SVS-9 17)

The Path:
Labour

Chennaiah, the cobbler:

After erecting three pillars
The gross, the subtle and the causal bodies.
After beating the buffaloes' rough hide
After removing the flesh
With the staff of the manifest and the hidden,
After tanning the hide with the fibre of dualism
After pouring the caustic juice of quintessence
Into the hide-pouch of awareness,
The blemishes of soul thus destroyed
I have come
To take the sandals to his feet.
Take care,
Not of the ground below,
But of the path your feet and sandals take.
Do not be enslaved
By the hand-awl, blade or peg
But realize
Ramarama, your own true self, the joy of joys!

(SPV 438)

Chennaiah, the cobbler:

Semen, blood, marrow, flesh,
Hunger, thirst, grief, sensuality
These are one and the same.
Only the trades of men are different
For the spirit that sees
Appearances are the same.
No matter what one's caste
Thanks to realization
One becomes absorbed in primal truth
And a kinsman of defilement and limitation
Through forgetfulness
Realizing both
I have never forgotten them.
Do not be enslaved
By the hand-awl, blade or peg
But realize
Ramarama, your own true self, the joy of joys!

(SPV 40)

Labour

Chennaiah, the cobbler:

When the wick and the oil together
Are touched by fire,
Of what is light composed?
Of the wick? Of the oil?
Or of the fire's essence?
The shining light
When the three come together
Is set ablaze by the wind.
When one sees
With the wisdom of embodied actions,
It is all form, no name—
How do you see?
With what feeling?
When will you be rid
Of the seeing of one thing dubiously
Through another?
Do not be enslaved
By the hand-awl, blade or peg
But realize
Ramarama, your own true self, the joy of joys!

(SPV-2 49)

Dhoolaiah, the cobbler:

On seeing the great godhead
Appear on the edge of the chisel
Piercing the hide—
'Why are you here, sir
In front of the one that moves about
Carrying the bag of flesh?
Go, go away
To the dwelling places of your devotees
Free them
Go on to the top of your silver mountain,
With your masquerades
Go free your devotees.
By the grace of the master of lust, dust and smoke
Go and prosper.

(SVS-8 422)

Dhoolaiah, the cobbler:

Everyone pierces the hide of cattle
With awareness.
Everyone pierces the hide of cattle
In forgetfulness.
But I pierce the hide
Of dead cattle.
I cut away the hide
And the truthful ones put sandals on
I expect them to show me
Emptiness
Take your paths, all of you
Mine is the path
Of the master of lust, dust and smoke.
That is enough for me.

(SPV 464)

Lakkamma, the rice gleaner:

That I have laboured to pick only rice—
Has the feeling dried up?
That I have done it—
Has the anxiety dried up?
When the wages of these two dry up
Amareshwaralinga, beloved of Marayya
Grows slack.

(SVS-5 199)

Lakkamma, the rice gleaner:

He alone is poor in things
Who is not pure in heart
But, for you who, pure in mind,
Performs his labour
Lakshmi appears wherever he looks
As long as you serve
Amareshwaralinga, beloved of Marayya.

(SVS-5 203)

Maritande, the clown:

The people that come
Riding on the backs of dancing horses
To watch many roles being played—
I saw their commotion
Was afraid
And hit myself.
O Mareshwara, foe of haste.

(VK 437)

Maritande, the burglar:

For the master of my picklock
I slaughtered a goat
Sacrificed a monkey
Dedicated my mother, my father.
If, in spite of all this,
The thing stolen
Does not come to me lovingly,
I declare—
Lord of Mara, the love god,
The foe of Mara
Does not exist!

(SPV-3 60)

Maritande, the burglar:

If I am a thief at night
That would be a shame
To the master who gave me the picklock.
If I enter houses
When people are forgetful
That would be a shame
To my expertise.
I wake up the forgetful,
Show them their riches
Then bring out my own riches, O Father
Lord of Mara, the love god
Foe of Mara.

(SPV-3 60)

Labour

Kannappa, the animal catcher:

I aimed three arrows
With the same bow.
I shot one, binding
Creation of the lotus-born
I shot another, binding
The hands of the lotus-navel
The last arrow
Pierced Rudra's forehead.

The blade broke
The plume fell away,
The arrow's cleft split
The bow held by Allama, Gogeshwara's Sharana
Was broken.

(SPV-3 103)

Ramanna, the cowherd:

At dawn,
I keep vigil of Brahma.
At noon
I keep vigil of Vishnu.
At sunset
I keep vigil of Rudra.
After dark
After driving the herd
Back to their folds ...
O when shall I be rid of this cowherd's staff?
No,
This cowherd's staff shall not drop
From my hands
Until Vishveshwaralinga, the lord of cattle,
Ceases to be.

(SPV-2 357)

Chowdaiah of many guises:

Entering from behind a nondescript curtain
Putting on many guises
Of the living
I was playing the form
Of the lord of all beasts
I shattered the amplifier
Tore up the curtain
Proclaiming—
Things living are nowhere in space!
I was hailing Naginatha, dear to Rekanna
Purahare . . .

(SPV-2 537)

Chowdaiah of many guises:

Donning eighty-four million disguises
In splendid forms
I came to amuse my kinsmen
They do not know
The beauty of many disguises
All the splendour
Of many disguises dissolves
Into formlessness
In Naginatha, dear to Rekanna.

(SPV-2 536)

Chowdaiah, the ferryman:

Here I come, a ferryman without a body
To the great flowing river
If you pay the price—
Your mind
That grasps and lets go,
I shall take you across
The great stream
To the end,
To the village
Without words or limits,
Says Chowdaiah, the ferryman.

(SVS-6 53)

The Path: Journey

Akkamahadevi:

You parrots, chirping on by rote!
Have you seen him? Have you?
You, koels, singing aloud!
Have you seen him? Have you?
You bees, swooping, sporting!
Have you seen him? Have you?
You swans sporting on lake's edge!
Have you seen him? Have you?
You hunting men and women
Sporting among hills and vales,
Have you seen him? Have you?
Where is he,
Channamallikarjuna, my god?
Tell me, won't you,
If you have seen ...

(MV 116)

Akkamahadevi:

You Hunger, stand still, stand still
You Thirst, stand still, stand still
You, Delusion, stand still, stand still
You, Lust, stand still, stand still,
You, Intoxication, stand still, stand still
You, Pride, you, Hate,
Stand still, stand still
All of you, still and moving,
Stand still, stand still
I am carrying an urgent letter
To my master, Channamallikarjuna.

Goodbye!

(MV 48)

Journey

Akkamahadevi:

Dear one,
Listen, if you like, like, or don't if you don't
I cannot live if I don't long for you,
Thrilled at your sight

Dear one,
Like me, if you like, or don't if you don't

Dear one,
Be pleased, if you like, or don't if you don't
I cannot live if I don't cherish you with delight

Dear Channamallikarjuna
I revel in the joy of adoring you,
Dear one.

(AV 58)

Akkamahadevi:

I had kept quiet
You were busy with the army and the fight
I had kept my cool
You had joined the army and the fight
How can I live
When you are in my hands, in my heart
But do not speak to me?
If she, this messenger,
Cannot win Channamallikarjuna,
Tell me O Mother
What shall I do
With her?

(AV 10)

Akkamahadevi:

I, a cow, came following a bull
I, a cow, came with faith, with trust
That he would nurse and protect me,
I came close to him
Hoping he would love me, love me.
O Father, Channamallikarjuna,
When someone else kidnapped
The woman who had come trusting you
How could you endure it,
O my god of gods?

(AGV 21)

Akkamahadevi:

You are my husband and I, your wife.
I have none else, O Lord

Falling in love with you, I came
I followed you.
When every passerby is grabbing my hands,
Tell me, O Husband,
How can you stand it?

O master Channamallikarjuna,
When strangers are dragging away
The woman leaning on your arms,
O king of compassionate ones,
Is it proper to stand aside and look on?

(AV 20)

Journey

Akkamahadevi:

The deer on earth and the hare in the moon—
What good is their love
If they cannot mate?
If your eyes lust in vain
It is like a mango tree
Bearing fruits
Standing in a flood.
O master Channamallikarjuna,
I came into a world I should not have come into
For I fell in love with the one too far away.

(AV 9)

Akkamahadevi:

When in passion
Do what you like, O Master
When in passion
Cut off the locks, O Master
When in passion
Bite off the fingers, O Master,
O master Channamallikarjuna
Heap miseries on me
If I ever grumble in pain.

(AV 9)

Journey

Akkamahadevi:

Don't hold me. Don't
Stop me. Let go
Of my hand, the hem
Of my sari. Don't
You know of the worst hell
For those that break
The promise made in black and white?
You shall be doomed
If you touch the woman
Married to Channamallikarjuna.

(AGV 53)

Akkamahadevi:

As waters of the body began to fill up,
The mind became a boat.

O Boatman,
Ferry me across smoothly.

O Boatman,
The hope is firm
That I will cross the tide.

Ferry me smoothly, O Boatman,
Channamallikarjuna of the hills of fortune.

(AV 48)

Journey

Allama Prabhu:

Darkness, the grasping hand, O Friend
Darkness, the seeing eye, O Friend
Darkness, the remembering heart, O Friend.
All darkness, two-headed, on this side, O Friend.
Gogeshwara's form,
His face turned away
Is on the other side, O Friend.

(AVC 51)

Allama Prabhu:

If I am not god,
Are you god?
If you are god,
Why do you not take care of me?
When thirsty, I offer myself a pitcher of water
When hungry, I give myself a morsel of rice
Look!
I am god, O Gogeshwara!

(AVC 123)

Journey

Allama Prabhu:

Whence the mango tree?
Whence the koel bird?
Whence, whence the kinship, O Brother?
The gooseberry on the mountains,
The salt from the sea:
Whence the kinship, O Brother
Whence, whence the kinship, O Brother,
Between us, Gogeshwara and me?

(AVC 15)

Allama Prabhu:

O my heart
Knowing no determination
You have made grief your food and drink,
Tell me, you,
What is this thread of maya?
The darkness within the eye
Does not grow clear.

O Gogeshwara
The splendour in the light
Is languishing.

(AVC 13)

Allama Prabhu:

When cinders rain down,
Be like the water.
When in the water deluge,
Be like the wind.
When in the great deluge,
Be like the sky.
When in the cosmic deluge,
Give yourself up,
Become Gogeshwara himself.

(AVC 122)

Basavanna:

You have spread before me
The green grass of lust, O Father.
What does the cow know?
It is drawn to the green.
O make me free from lust
Make me drink the juice of your devotion
Bathe me in waters of pure knowledge
Save me
O Kudalasangama.

(BSV 14)

Basavanna:

For the chakora bird,
The longing after moonlight;
For the lotus,
The longing after sunrise;
For the bee,
The longing after sweet nectar;
But, for me,
Only the longing
For the coming of Kudalasangama.

(BSV 91)

Basavanna:

I am spotted like the moon
The wicked serpent of the world
Has swallowed me whole, O Father.
Today,
My body has been eclipsed.
When will I be free?
O Kudalasangamadeva.

(SVS-1 6)

Basavanna:

Moon rise:
The ocean in full tide.
The moon wanes:
The ocean ebbs away.
When Rahu obstructs the moon,
Does the ocean shout aloud?
When the sage drinks the ocean,
Does the moon get in his way?
There is no one for anyone
No place for the fallen
Except you O Father
O kinsman of the whole world
O Kudalasangamadeva.

(BSV 8)

Basavanna:

The elephant is huge
Can you say, 'The driver's hook is small?'
No Father, you cannot.

The mountain is huge
Can you say, 'The lightning bolt is small?'
No Father, you cannot.

Darkness is immense
Can you say, 'The lamp is small?'
No Father, you cannot.

Forgetfulness is immense
Can you say, 'The heart that remembers you is small?'
No Father, O Kudalasangamadeva,
You cannot.

(BSV 3)

Basavanna:

Is the swollen wave of the ocean of the world
Playing about my face?
Tell me
Has the ocean of the world risen to my chest?
Tell me
Has the ocean of the world risen to my throat?
Tell me
What can I say
When the ocean of the world is rising over my head?
O! O! Hear me howl O Father! O Father!
Kudalasangama
Whhhhhh ... what can I do?

(BSV 4)

Basavanna:

Before the bearded chin turns grey
And the cheeks wrinkle,
The body turns into a cage ...
Before the teeth fall away,
The back is bent,
And you are dependent on others
Before one hand rests on your knee,
And another holds a stick
Before age disfigures the frame
Before death touches you,
Worship him, our master Kudalasangama.

(BSV 42)

Basavanna:

I have caged the bird, oiled the lamp,
Got the wick ready,
I am waiting for his coming, O Mother.
When dry leaves rustle I look out, listening,
My abandoned heart begins to rage, O Mother.
When devotees of Kudalasangamadeva
Stand at the door, saying 'Shiva'
How happy I become, O Mother!

(BSV 94)

Basavanna:

When you speak
Your words must be
Like a string of pearls, the glow of ruby:
Crystal clear, needle sharp.
When you speak,
Linga, pleased, must say,
'Quite so, quite so.'
When speech does not square with deeds,
How can he be pleased,
Kudalasangamadeva?

(BSV 218)

Journey

Basavanna:

Can there be faith
Without loving kindness, O Brother?
There must be loving kindness
For every living creature, O Brother.

Loving kindness
Is the root of all faith, O Brother
O Kudalasangamadeva.

(BSV 63)

Basavanna:

I am just one person
But there are five of them
Burning me.

When a tiger is dragging
The wild bull away,
Can you not rescue it
O master Kudalasangama?

(BSV 35)

Basavanna:

Look, all of you,
The world of god and the world of men
Are not different.
Speaking truth is the world of god
Telling lies is the world of humans
Virtue is heaven
And vice, hell.
O master Kudalasangama,
You are my witness.

(VK 47)

Basavanna:

So hard to practise, this devotion
Like a saw, it cuts coming and going,
Will a king cobra not strike
At the hand thrust near it,
O master Kudalasangama?

(BSV 54)

Basavanna:

Her words are like jaggery
But in her heart is poison
Look, O Father,
She calls one with her eyes,
Thinks of another in her mind.
Listen, O father Kudalasangama
Don't you trust this false-hearted thief
Of men's hearts.

(BSV–LB 111)

Goggavve:

Like fragrance blending with breeze
Like pleasure blending with lovemaking
Like the quality of giving in admiration—

This, I say, is the path for devotees.

(VS 318)

Revanasiddha:

Ten types of melody have been heard
In ten directions, have they not?
Flowers have bloomed
Auspiciously, have they not?
Great joy has come
To all peoples, has it not?
Has he not come yet—
The destroyer of three cities,
The master of the moon?

(vs 40)

Dhoolaiah, the cobbler:

Lust means
'Craving for'
Smoke means
'Darkness rising from it.'
He, made of dust
Ground both into dust
And became the master of dust.

(SPV 465)

Dhoolaiah, the cobbler:

Like a lightning creeper
Like a roar in the sky
Like a bubble
Like the riches of coral
That appears in a dream—
The attitude unattached to these,
That of your own self,
The anarchist, uncommitted
Without faith
Freed of the defiling touch of the mean
Attached to none, nothing,
The master of lust, dust and smoke.

(SPV 459)

Siddharama:

When lines combine with lines
Letters are formed
When letters combine with letters
Words are formed
When words combine with words
Many books are formed:
But Kapilasiddhamallikarjuna
Is not,
In the lines, words,
Letters or many books
He is nothing, he never was.
'He is' 'he is not'
Both these statements take nothing
Away from him.
Great, his vastness.

(VK 78)

Siddharama:

Release me from dreams, O Master,
For I am tied down with ropes in dreams
O master Kapilasiddhamallikarjuna.

(SSV 23)

Dasimaiah, the weaver:

You are, O Three-eyed One,
Like a thread among pearls
Different, the bodies when counted
But, one and the same, the soul.
Realizing that you dwell
Full of attributes
In the smallest of atoms and particles,
Blades of grass and wood
I adore you, O Ramanatha.

(DDV 55)

Lingamma, the virtuous wife of
Hadapada Appanna:

The mind grows dull
The body vanishes
The breath stops
The flame appears
The smoke spreads
The lake is all burnt down.
Unless you go in,
Open the door
And immerse yourself in light
There is no true freedom,
Said Channabasavanna, dear to Appanna.

(SVS-5 255)

Molige Mahadevi:

Having strung six pearls together
O the learned philosophers are looking for
A pearl for the final knot
The work of each beginning
Wisdom of the eternal
The moment the difference is understood
The pearl for the final knot appears
The moment he is said to be one,
The beloved of my lord Mallikarjunalinga
Of two-fold purity.

(SVS-5 284)

Molige Mahadevi:

When you give me shelter,
You become formless giving up the investigation of forms
You become powerless, unattached
Giving up the company of your power.
You become free from worry
Giving up the sense of quantity
That aims at looking into the heart.
Shed the guise of deceit and humbug
You have put on
To examine the hearts of other devotees
Become free from all passions,
Endowed with all virtues
Full like the ocean of wisdom.
Just once, open for me the temple of your awareness.
You will see the affinity between
My feet and your temple
No more humbug in this:
O beloved of my lord, Mallikarjuna
Of two-fold purity.

(SVS-5 285)

Remmavve, the spinner:

Other men are heroes
In the army outside
My man, a hero
In the army inside.
Other men hunt elephants
My man, the heart
Other men earn and get fed
Other men have three
My man has just one
Even that is doubtful
O Gummeshwara, lord of the spool.

(SPV-3 57)

Gajesha Masanaiah:

When I saw him
I forgot the eight directions, O Mother.
O Mother, Mother
When I got him to speak to me
My entire body broke into sweat
What next, O Mother?
Today when Mahalinga Gajeshwara
Is embracing me
I have forgotten
To embrace him ...
What next, O Mother?

(SPV-2 190)

Ghattivalaiah:

Look, all of you
At this plant of sorrow
Look, all of you
At my sowing it in the pariahs' street.
If you pour on it water
Of the water bearer
I will pluck from the plant
The bloom of desire
And adorn the love god with it
O Siddalinga, dear to Chikkaiah
O never, never.

(SPV 255)

Journey

Ghattivalaiah:

Unless
You go away after being born
Unless
You return after going away
Who will sense the emptiness inside the sound?
Tell me
Who else will see the place
Where Siddalinga, dear to Chikkaiah
Both is and is not!

(SPV 241)

Nilambike:

I can't be called Basava's wife
Neither can Basava be called my man.
Tearing apart the kinship of two-ness
I became Basava's infant
And Basava, my infant
Shiva's warriors and devotees of old
Are my witnesses
Without violating the ordeal
Set by Sangaiah
I have hidden myself in Basava.

(SVS-5 260)

Nilambike:

You left me O Basava, O my master
In dense forest
You ravaged O Basava, O my master
The middle of the village
You grant children O Basava, O my master
To a barren woman
You denied her O Basava, O my master
The contentment of having those children.
How glorious you are O Basava, O my master
In Sangaiah.

(SVS-5 236)

Bommaiah, the drum beater:

You who tasted the milk
From three breasts
Saw ten states
Tell me, who are you?
It's a pity you came
To the undivided town
To suffer pain
Your past, forgotten,
Now a victim of doubt.
Know the gap between the two states—
Your own self, O Bheemeshwaralinga.
O bodiless companion
Burning of the forest of good deeds.

(SVS-7 284)

The Destination: Union

Akkamahadevi:

O Sister, listen Sister dear
I dreamt a dream. I saw
Rice, betel and coconut
I saw, O dear
A gorava boy
With short matted locks of hair
And shining teeth
Coming home for alms
I went chasing him
Going beyond all boundaries
And held his hands
Seeing Channamallikarjuna, I opened
My eyes.

(MV 112)

Akkamahadevi:

Guru became kin,
Linga, the bridegroom
And I, the bride.
The whole world knows:
The uncountable devotees are my parents
Who gave me in marriage
Finding the ideal groom

Channamallikarjuna is my husband,
No one else
O Brother

(AGV 54)

Akkamahadevi:

Like treasure hiding in the earth
Like taste hiding in the fruit
Like gold hiding in the stone
Like oil hiding in sesame
Like fire hiding in the tree
No one can see Channamallikarjuna—
The Brahman hiding in yearning.

(MV 3)

Akkamahadevi:

You are the whole forest
You are all the divine trees in the forest
You are all the birds and beasts
Sporting amidst trees
O Channamallikarjuna,
Though all is filled with you
Why don't you show me your face
Turned away from me?

(MV 140)

Akkamahadevi:

Show me, quick,
How to be one with you
Do not throw me out
I, a slave meant for you,
Have come to you
Do not throw me out
O master Channamallikarjuna
I have come close to you
To rely on you
Take me in, quick.

(AV 34)

Akkamahadevi:

The clear light of the sun
The sky's expanse
The movement of breeze
The leaves, flowers,
Trees, bushes and creepers—
Seven colours.
These, the splendours of the day.
The glow of the moon,
Stars, lightning and so on,
All things glowing,
Your worship at night.

Day and night
I lose myself in your worship
O Channamallikarjuna.

(MV 129)

Akkamahadevi:

To him with no death,
No decay
No form

To the beautiful one
I have given myself O Mother.

To him with no place
No end
No space
No signs

To the beautiful one
I have given myself O Mother.

To him with no clan
No country,
To the peerless
Handsome one
I have given myself O Mother.

For this reason
Channamallikarjuna, the handsome one
Is the man for me.
These wasting, dying men—
Take them away
Throw them into the oven!

(VK 61)

Allama Prabhu:

The bee-flower is blossoming on the plant.
Watch the bee, filled with bliss
Watch the soul-bee, filled with bliss
Watch the bee, god-bee, filled with bliss
Bowing down to Gogeshwara, the Linga,
The bee is filled, full of awe.
Look!

(APV 119)

Union

Allama Prabhu:

When the unseen guru appears to the eye
Unspoken prayers
Untouched touch of the palm and the forehead
Unworn marks of the holy ash
Unheard mantra in the ears
Holy bath from the sacred vessels
Not filled or overflowing.
Initiation without scriptures
Unworshippable Linga
O Gogeshwara
Let me receive the grace
Of kinship without togetherness,
Becoming the self.

(AVC 166)

Basavanna:

Listen you, man-hero, listen.
Only for your sake, I wear a man's garb.
Once again I am a man
Once again I am a woman
O Kudalasangamadeva
O master at the confluence
I am a man-hero for you
And a bride for your devotees.

(BSV 187)

Union

Basavanna:

Never heard
Of tunes or rhythms
Or kept count of cymbal beats
Never about feet
Ambrosial or divine.

O master Kudalasangama,
Because no harm can ever come to you
I sing as I please.

(BSV 3)

Basavanna:

When a pond or pool or well goes dry
Bubbles, shells and shards can be seen.
When the ocean goes dry
Diamonds can be seen.
When Kudalasangama's devotees
Lay bare their hearts and speak
Linga can be seen.

(BSV 265)

Basavanna:

Is the world of men
Different from the world of god?
Within this very world
Endless worlds—
Shiva's world means
Shiva's virtues.
The world of god is
Where the devotee is
The devotee's courtyard
Is Varanasi.
The body, Kailasa
This is the truth,
O Kudalasangamadeva.

(BSV 47)

Basavanna:

Having filled my speech
With the heavenly nectar of your name
My eyes, with your form
My heart, with your memory
My ears, with your hymns

O Kudalasangamadeva
I am a bee
Fulfilled by your lotus feet.

(BSV 33)

Bonthadevi:

The emptiness in the body
The emptiness in the monastery
Empty, empty, emptiness . . .
Emptiness, the whole of one's self
O Emptiness, carefree!

(SVS-5 1269)

Urilingadeva:

In my great rapture
Of making love with my darling
I can't tell myself from the world.
While making love with my love
I can't tell myself from my darling
After making love with Urilingadeva
The god of the burning member
I can't tell whether it is me, him
Or something else.

(VK 393)

Gajesha Masanaiah:

As if touched by the autumn grass
My mother was thrilled.
Her words came faltering
She lived,
His love her sole source of strength.
Like a white bee sucking
Nectar in vermilion dust,
She was absorbed in her own self
In Mahalinga Gajeshwara.

(SPV–2 192)

Nilambike:

Long ago an infant was born.
A ruby placed in its hands
Appeared, in many-coloured
And then took refuge
In emptiness,
For Basava
Whose name is lost in Sangaiah.

(SVS-5 263)